INTRODUCTION

'HE IS NOT ONLY the wisest man alive but has been the most generous in his offerings to the immortals who live in heaven.'

'I am Odysseus, Laertes' son. The whole world talks of my stratagems, and my fame has reached the heavens... The same wind as wafted me from Ilium brought me to Ismarus, the city of the Cicones. I sacked this place and destroyed the men who held it. The wives and the rich plunder that we took from the town we divided so that no-one, as far as I could help it, should go short of his proper share ... [on the land of the Cyclopes] my men's first idea was to make off with some of the cheeses, then come back, drive the kids and lambs quickly out of the pens to the good ship, and so set sail across the water... we lit a fire, killed a beast and made offerings ... [on Aeaea, the land of Circe] I went with the goddess to her beautiful bed.'

'The bright-eyed goddess smiled at Odysseus' tale and caressed him with her hand ... "And so my stubborn friend, Odysseus the arch-deceiver, with his cunning for intrigue, does not propose in his own country to drop his sharp practice and the lying tales that he loves from the bottom of his heart".'[1]

So runs the tale of Odysseus, beloved of the gods for his cunning and prowess; willing to rape and pillage, to take for his own, and to sleep with any woman if she were but beautiful enough; praised for deeds that today we call indefensible. What made the difference? What took us from a culture that praises men for war, theft, rape, adultery, and deceit, to one that holds these things in abhorrence? Who, or what, told us that these things are wrong, and such people are not heroes to be put on pedestals and praised for their cunning and valour?

According to historians like Tom Holland and Christians like Glen Scrivener, the difference is Christianity. It is Christianity that told us that we should not just love ourselves, our family, and our tribe but also our enemy. It is Christianity that told us that the greatest person is not the one who fights the hardest and has the most self-directed cunning, but the person who gets on their knees and serves. It is Christianity that tells us that leaders are not gods, but servants; that their position is not to make themselves rich, but to enrich their people. It is Christianity that has transformed the Western world and politics.

And yet, it is easy to find people who say that religion has no place in politics. Carrying out an internet search for the phrase results in multiple cases of people agreeing with or arguing in favour of the statement. It even comes up on Reddit.[2] Sam Dowler, writing for the *Huffington Post*, says that, 'While religion plays a huge part in many people's lives, they recognise that it's not appropriate to bring it up in certain aspects of life.'[3] He says that religion in politics is 'completely counter-productive' and 'religion should be kept as far away from politics as possible'. Rosie Duthie says that 'religion in politics is derisive'.[4] Andrew Scott heads up an article with the title, 'No place for God in British politics',[5] while Sam Killerman goes for the title,

'I'm not anti-Christian, but religion shouldn't have a place in political decisions' and categorises the blog-post as 'an article about social justice'.[6]

Proponents of this argument want politics to be based on reason and argument, and feel that religion and religious views are antithetical to this. But it is by no means agreed that objective morality is possible, let alone superior, without God. It is arguable, even, that the best politics is impossible without religion, because there is no way of deciding that certain acts (e.g. advocating violence against disabled people, Black people, right-wing people, etc.) are intrinsically wrong or morally permissible.

It can, therefore, be argued that there is no decent, moral, defensible, and objectively right politics without religion. Without an objective standard outside of ourselves, we have no reason for saying that Odysseus is to be pilloried as a pillager and adulterer, rather than praised as a hero and champion. For Christians,[7] it is God, through the Bible, who is the ultimate arbiter of morals.

It can also be argued that politics is integral to religion. Religions advocate certain worldviews that have implications for how societies should be structured, economies run, and people treated. Christianity, in particular, has influenced Western society to the extent that political views considered untenable in pre-Christian times and places are now assumed as obviously correct in post-Christian countries. These include the importance of looking after people who are not only not part of your family, tribe, or in-group, but to whom you are violently or diametrically opposed; humility as a virtue versus the greed, violence, and hubris of Odysseus and other Greek and Roman 'heroes'; and forgiveness rather than permanent exclusion. Contrast these virtues with neoliberal politics and neo-classical economics, in which greed and the encouragement of inequality of income are virtues to be celebrated and encouraged; or extremes of left or right cultural values where the other is to be condemned, shut down, and driven out. There is no unconditional love, tolerance, humility, or forgiveness in these positions, yet they are allowed to inform and influence political positions.

Worldviews help us to think about not just what outcomes we want to achieve but how to achieve them. Worldviews are integral to politics and any understandings of what to value and how to attain what we value, and religion-based worldviews are no more inherently wrong or right than atheistic and humanistic worldviews (leaving aside for now that there either is a particular deity/deities or not).

Christianity as a worldview has a lot to say to and about politics. Christianity says that, in the interests of justice and generosity, we should all be on the side of the poor and oppressed against the rich and oppressive. But Christianity also says that the poor and the oppressed are equally capable of sin and of oppressing others; poor people are not good by virtue of being poor. As Aleksandr Solzhenitsyn says, 'The line separating good and evil passes not through states, nor between classes, nor between political parties either – but right through every human heart – and through all human hearts.'[8] If he is correct – and the Bible would say that he is – then this has political implications that cannot be avoided by such simplistic tropes as 'religion has no place in politics'.

For Christians, the principles and virtues that God laid down in the Bible are not just to inform how Christians live, but how all people live. When God judges people at the end of this age, he will judge us for the failure to live up to his principles as he revealed them to us, regardless of whether we acknowledge him as Lord or not. That is part of what sin is: the failure to obey God; the decision to disobey him; the harm and injustice caused by our greed and oppression of others contrary to God's law. The books of the prophets declare God's anger and judgment against pagan nations for their oppression and injustice. God demands just politics; just processes; just people.

Indeed, I think that politics is so important to God that worship is not just incomplete but becomes a stench to him without the political virtues of justice and generosity. Lives of justice and generosity are a part of our worship to God, without which the rest of our worship – the formulaic, ritualistic aspects of singing, prayer, Bible reading, and corporate gathering – are just superstitious cults that become blasphemous.

One of the questions I seek to answer in this book is how did the laws that God gave the Israelites lead to human flourishing and salvation, and how do we apply the same underpinning principles to achieve the same goals today, in our context? In particular, I am writing in the context of the UK, which has (albeit in increasingly denuded form since the 1980s, and in particular since 2010) a welfare state, and a basic appreciation of the role of government in caring for all UK citizens. But it is one thing to understand what God told the Israelites several thousand years ago. It is another to then determine what that means for how we should live today; what are the practical implications for us?

Oliver O'Donovan discusses hermeneutics in his book *Self, World and Time: Ethics as Theology 1*. He writes,

A biblical story, command or counsel presents us with a train of moral thought, a discursive argument that runs, though sometimes we need exegetical insight to make it explicit, from some [situation] A to some [action] B, led by its practical question, observing some contextual constraints and reaching some resolution. That whole course of thinking, from A to B, is laid before our attention as we seek to fashion a course of thinking of our own, from some [situation] X to some [action] Y, led by our own practical question, observing our own contextual restraints, and finally reaching our own resolution of the matter that is in our own view… Obedience is a matter of how our own confession is to harmonise with the testimony of Scripture, and it is concerned to achieve a correspondence between the *whole train of thought* of the text from A to B and the *whole* train of thought from X to Y… Nothing will count as 'biblical' thinking but a careful correlation of the complexities of the one situation with the complexities of the other.[9]

William Witt explains how, according to sixteenth-century theologian Richard Hooker,

not every 'positive' law in Scripture is a matter for permanent observance. The interpreter had to discern the purpose of the positive law in its original context, whether it was rooted in 'natural' or 'moral' law, or was rather of merely historical relevance, and where it fits within the context of both creation and redemption. For example, the civil laws of the Old Testament would not be binding on modern states, although the moral principles behind them are …

One has not understood the logic of any biblical command until one has understood how the moral principle of the law is rooted in the ontology of creation and redemption, and the teleological purpose behind the law. How does the law lead to human flourishing and salvation?[10]

Many theologians shy away from any form of political application of theological principles, noting that, as theologians, they do not have a background in politics. They often have not looked at the empirical evidence for different policies, so might be able to note certain principles but can't comment on whether any given policy or political approach meets those principles. I have a background in welfare and disability, so in this book I use my knowledge of these policies and approaches to economic and social justice, to make suggestions on how biblical principles might be applied in the UK today. This is context specific: a very different country, such as Japan, might approach things very differently; the US, however, may still find these suggestions helpful because the US is similar (but often harsher) to the UK in its approach to poverty and people in need.

CHAPTER 1
WHY WE WORSHIP GOD

HAVE YOU EVER BEEN in a cathedral, particularly one of Gothic architecture, and wondered at its awe and majesty? The soaring heights; the strong and mighty walls; the glorious stained-glass windows; the intricate mouldings. Then there's the peace; the sense of eternity; the remembrance that this is a place where people have come for centuries to talk to God and to pour out their hopes, thanks, and sufferings. There are few places that I find as inspiring and encouraging as a building dedicated to God, displaying his characteristics, and filled with the memories of centuries of worship.

A cathedral can point us to many of God's characteristics and remind us, at times when we are overwhelmed or rushed off our feet, why we worship him. There is the strength and thickness of the walls, reminding us of God's strength; the depth of the foundations, pointing us to the dependency of our trust in God; the durability of the building, which even when neglected for years still has walls standing. The sheer space reflects the room that God has for all people, and the cross-based floor-plan centres the crucifixion and the salvation that God offers to all who will place their faith in him.

Even the decadence of the building points me back to God. There's an element of the alabaster jar in these buildings; of the woman who broke a jar of expensive perfume over Jesus' feet, prompting his response that 'wherever this gospel is preached throughout the world, what she has done will also be told, in memory of her'.[11] I do find myself retaining a degree of the Judas spirit, wondering about the value of building a cathedral to a God whose temple is now distributed in the bodies of his followers, when suffering people were in need of houses. But if we questioned every motive of our heart, we would never achieve anything; if we only acted when there was unambiguous good, we would never do anything. The fact remains that at least some people built cathedrals with the intention of glorifying God and assisting worshippers to glorify God; and in that spirit, and in memory of all the people who have worshipped and sought God there, I will continue to enjoy the reminder of God that cathedrals can bring.

This reminder is central to my life. It is easy, in Christianity, to fall into one of two camps: our behaviour does not matter, because we cannot earn salvation; or our behaviour must conform to all of God's standards. We may even find that we take both positions at once, treating obedience to some of God's laws as central to salvation and others as unnecessary. We may be legalistic on sexual morality, purity, and chastity, whilst stressing the need to not be legalistic when it comes to critiquing our western lifestyles, greed, inequality, and selfishness. Or we may view things the other way around: we may be relaxed when it comes to traditional Christian views on sexual morality, whilst critiquing the power dynamics, oppression, and greed of Western culture. Either way, we are treating some issues with undue laxity whilst becoming inappropriately legalistic on others.

To avoid both legalism and laxity, I have found the desire to glorify God to be a helpful motivating force in my life. When I reflect on the glory and awesomeness of God, and all that he has done for me, then I find myself wanting others to recognise just how amazing God is. I want them to admit the greatness of his character and who he is. I am inspired to live in line with God's character, so that people may 'see my good deeds and glorify my Father in heaven'.[12] That is why, when I think about what is right to do, I start with remembering how and why I worship God. This is the driving force that keeps me joyful whilst avoiding both laxity and legalism.

WHY WE ARE TO PRAISE GOD

The Westminster Catechism says that man's chief and highest end is to glorify God and enjoy him forever. We were made to live lives that bring honour and praise to God, and in which we honour and praise God. It is central to who we are as Christians.

The Bible is full of such commands:

'He is the one you praise; he is your God, who performed for you those great and awesome wonders you saw with your own eyes.'[13]

'Ascribe to the Lord, all you families of nations, ascribe to the Lord glory and strength. Ascribe to the Lord the glory due his name; bring an offering and come before him. Worship the Lord in the splendour of his holiness.'[14]

'Speak to one another with psalms, hymns, and songs from the Spirit. Sing and make music from your heart to the Lord, always giving thanks to God the Father for everything, in the name of our Lord Jesus Christ.'[15]

21

WE PRAISE GOD BECAUSE OF HIS NATURE

The Westminster Catechism says that 'God is a Spirit, in and of himself infinite in being, glory, blessedness, and perfection; all-sufficient, eternal, unchangeable, incomprehensible, everywhere present, almighty, knowing all things, most wise, most holy, most just, most merciful and gracious, long-suffering, and abundant in goodness and truth.' If you ever need a reason to praise God, this is a great place to start!

When Moses asks God who he should say has sent him, God tells him to say that 'I am' is sending him, meaning that God exists in and of himself.[16] God was there when nothing else, not even time, existed, and he owes his existence to nothing and no-one. Indeed, so far from being created by or dependent upon anything else, the whole of creation – everything that exists that is not God – was created by and depends upon him. This tells us some other things: he is almighty because it is by his power that everything was created and is sustained, and nothing created or sustains God; he is unchangeable, because there is nothing that can change him; he is eternal, because nothing exists that could end him.

The word Paul used in 1 Timothy 1:11 and 6:15 to describe God as 'blessed' can also be translated as 'happy'. It is a funny word, as we are used to using 'blessed' to mean someone who has received good things in life, especially from God. But God doesn't bless himself with good things! Rather, 'blessed' means that God is completely happy, fulfilled, and content in himself. He doesn't need anyone or anything to make him happy.

The Bible is full of praise for God for the wondrous nature of his being, and we do well to include these features in our songs of worship. Daniel says, 'Praise be to the name of God for ever and ever; wisdom and power are his'.[17] David declares, 'how majestic is Your name in all the earth!'[18] and 'His greatness no-one can fathom'.[19] Paul reminds us that God 'is able to do immeasurably more than all we ask or imagine'.[20]

Creation is an inspiration to many, showing in the interweaving of rocks, climate, plants, and animals in a web of reciprocity the beauty of a master craftsman's handiwork. David sings of the heavens declaring God's glory, pouring forth the majesty of God to all.[21] Isaiah urges us to 'lift your eyes and look to the heavens' as we consider God's great power and mighty strength in the creation and sustainment of myriads of stars.[22] Works of art, like the cathedrals built to worship God, bring out the creative nature built into us by God, as well as attempting to reflect some of God's glory back to him.

We praise God also for his utter holiness. When the prophet Isaiah and apostle John saw glimpses of heaven, they saw the seraphim singing 'holy, holy, holy is the Lord God' over and over again.[23] God's holiness is a central and awe-inspiring part of who he is, which we cannot fully comprehend. Baker's Encyclopaedia of the Bible says that, 'the primary Old Testament word for holiness means "to cut" or "to separate". Fundamentally, holiness is a cutting off or separation from what is unclean, and a consecration to what is pure (sanctification).' The holiness is acquired because God himself is holy; he is what holiness means. God's holiness is a core reason why he should be worshipped. When I am in a cathedral, the centuries of prayer and worship that have happened there can bring a sense of that holiness of God, as though God's presence is fuller in places where so many people have sought and met with him.

WE PRAISE GOD FOR HIS CHARACTER

We know that God is perfect, for we are called to be perfect just as he is perfect – and we could not do that if he were not perfect! Calling God perfect means that what he says is true and what he does is right. For him to be able to always be right and true, he must be the essence of goodness and truth. He must know all things and be most wise in his use of that knowledge, and he must be all powerful, so that he is always able to overcome evil and never has to compromise with the 'least bad' option.

God's goodness means that he is perfectly just and will one day restore everything to its right state or place. God's goodness also means that he is full of mercy, grace, and patience. This is married to his justice through the death of Jesus – the penalty for sin was paid, meaning that all things can be restored to their rightful place, at the same time as God showed mercy (not giving people the punishment they deserve) and grace (giving people good things that they don't deserve). God's patience and desire to show mercy and grace to all means that he is waiting for as many people as possible to repent before he restores creation to its rightful state.

There are many verses in the Bible which declare God's character to us. These show us that God is both just and loving. God specifically says that he carries out justice for the poor[24] and oppressed,[25] and that he himself is just, upright, and true, never taking sides or being partial.[26] God's love is steadfast and everlasting;[27] so fervent that he himself died in order that we could choose to come back to him;[28] and patient, as he wants no-one to perish who might in time turn to him. God's love is all-powerful; nothing can keep it from us if only we accept his death in our place.[29]

Whatever we think of the motivations behind the construction of cathedrals, and whether or not we think that these cathedrals – or perhaps the palaces and mansions of the rich – should have been set aside in favour of building houses and other property for the poor, we know that God himself is concerned for the poor and for their wellbeing. When you think of the provisions that he laid out in the Law and the guarantees he makes for the future, it is clear that God's concern is not for the wealthy to be free to keep their wealth, but for everyone to have enough to enjoy and participate in society. God's character is one of justice and concern for the wellbeing of all people, and this is good.

WE PRAISE GOD FOR WHAT HE HAS DONE FOR US

God has rescued us from eternal death and separation from him, and allowed us to return to him as his children as if we had never left him at all. This can't be underestimated. Those people who continue to reject God will be 'shut out from the presence of the Lord and from the glory of his might.'[30] If you don't know God, then you may not realise what you're missing out on. But after death, you will realise. There will be 'weeping and gnashing of teeth'[31] for those who have not turned back to God. This is what God has rescued us from.

For those who have accepted Jesus as Lord and Saviour, we will enter the new heavens and earth, where we will live forever enjoying and worshipping God, in the eternal presence of God. Heaven will shine with the glory of God. It will be a place of peace, with no fighting or discord, and no contention, oppression, or poverty.[32] We will all have new, perfect, and glorious bodies[33] and there will be no suffering or tears. The Bible describes heaven in rich terms: streets of gold; walls of jewels; a tree-lined, clear-as-crystal river.[34]

Whilst still on earth, God provides for everyone, whether they follow him or not. God shows common grace to all through the ordinary miracles of the sun and rain, stable government, and smooth-running manufacturing and transport systems. When the Israelites were wandering in the desert, God provided water, manna, and quail for them.[35] He ensured that each person had enough manna for that day: no-one needed to collect more for the next (working) day, because God would provide that day's manna on that day. And God ensured that no-one needed to work to the extent that they never rested, or relied on their own strength rather than God's provision: the day before the Sabbath rest, God provided double manna, so that no-one needed to collect food on the Sabbath.

For those who follow him, and often in answer to prayer, God may intervene with extraordinary miracles. Sometimes he enables people to survive without basic necessities; other times he prompts others to give what is needed at the crucial moment; still other times God directly creates or multiplies provision such as food. Sometimes, God acts to enable his people to retain trust in and obedience to him, even as he seems to betray them by not providing for immediate needs or saving lives; this is perhaps the greatest miracle he can do, as he did for Job. God still loves us even as we experience the natural consequences of living in a broken, frustrated world with sinful people and active forces of darkness. God will ultimately rescue all who believe in and obey him – and for some that rescue is through death.[36]

God watches over us and helps us in times of trouble. Sometimes God smooths the way or breaks through obstacles that, prior to his intervention, appeared insurmountable and impregnable. Sometimes it may be that God permits these obstacles precisely so that we can see his power in overcoming them.[37] Although he does not prevent every difficult circumstance or harmful event, he is able to bring good out of even the worst of situations. Sometimes this is in terms of our character and relationship with God; a 'thorn in the side' can be the prompt that we fallible humans so often need to keep us looking to God rather than depending upon ourselves. Perhaps a difficult situation puts us in a place where we can serve God more than we ever dreamed of: the apostle Paul's imprisonment prevented him from going on missionary trips but meant that he wrote a substantial proportion of the New Testament. A whole range of gains can come from initially negative situations, often ones that we had not thought of. Many people find that, having come out the other side of a difficult situation, they wouldn't go back and change it.

At the very least, trials and difficulties can lead to a closer, purer, and tighter relationship with God. We learn more of who he is and who we are, and are purified – sanctified – of sin. Having already justified us – determined to view us as if we had never sinned – God is not satisfied with leaving us at that; he works in and with us to make us holy in practice as well as in status. Difficult times can help us to discover what our hearts are really like: the things we refused to let go of for God; the sins we run to; the goals we idolise. God already knows of the problems in our heart, but we often don't – and difficult times can be what reveals them to us so that, through

God's grace and with his help, we can overcome them.

Looking back on past situations, we can find many reasons to praise God. We praise him for our salvation and our future inheritance; for his provision of our daily necessities; for his overcoming of forces outside of our control; and for his use of daily life to remove the dross and dirt in our hearts, leaving us ever more refined and closer to him.

WE PRAISE GOD BECAUSE HE TOLD US TO

Finally, we praise God because he has commanded us to. In Deuteronomy, the Israelites are told, 'Circumcise your hearts, therefore, and do not be stiff-necked any longer… Fear the Lord your God and serve him. Hold fast to him and take your oaths in his name. He is the one you praise.'[38]

There are a number of places in the Bible that give us this command to worship God. The Psalms are a rich source of both commands to praise God and the praise itself. And in 1 Chronicles, King David says (or sings), 'Give praise to the Lord, proclaim his name; make known among the nations what he has done. Sing to him, sing praise to him; tell of all his wonderful acts. Glory in his holy name; let the hearts of those who seek the Lord rejoice… Sing to the Lord, all the earth; proclaim his salvation day after day. Declare his glory among the nations, his marvellous deeds among all peoples. For great is the Lord and most worthy of praise; he is to be feared above all gods… Ascribe to the Lord, all you families of nations, ascribe to the Lord glory and strength. Ascribe to the Lord the glory due his name; bring an offering and come before him. Worship the Lord in the splendour of his holiness.'[39]

Jesus clearly expected that believers would worship

him, telling the Samaritan woman that a time was coming and had come 'when the true worshippers will worship the Father in the Spirit and in truth, for are they are the kind of worshippers the Father seeks'.[40] The apostle John records this meeting in his gospel after the event of Jesus clearing the temple and declaring that he could restore the Temple in three days if it were destroyed. John clarifies for us that 'the temple he had spoken of was his body'.[41] The point is that the Jewish form of worship had become distorted – the place of worship had been turned into an oppressive market that cheated the people and blocked them from worshipping God. Jesus had come to remove all barriers between man and God.

In this passage, the visit from Nicodemus, and the meeting with a Samaritan woman, Jesus taught us that the mode of worship was changing. Worship would no longer be at the Temple or centred on ritual – things it was never meant to be anyway. Instead, worship would be praise of Jesus (instead of at the temple) and through God's empowering Spirit (instead of through the ritual of sacrifice, etc.).

Unlike most other religions at the time, the Jews had only one temple to God. This temple represented the dwelling place of God, and Jerusalem was his holy city. The Jews considered that the only proper place for worship, and for the sacrifices of the Jewish religion, was the Temple. In contrast, the Samaritans had since the time of Solomon's death sought to worship God by worshipping false idols in Dan and Beersheba.[42]

When the Samaritan woman asked Jesus whether Jerusalem was the only place where God could be worshipped, Jesus' reply was that, in essence, the question was no longer relevant. A new way of interacting with God was being introduced, which overrode both the

Jewish and the Samaritan religions (the Samaritans used only the first five books of the Old Testament and thought that they represented the true Israelites from which Judah and Benjamin broke away). It is at this point that Jesus says that true worshippers will worship God in spirit and truth. In this context, it becomes clear that Jesus was talking about the new covenant with God (Abraham's spiritual descendants; salvation through Jesus, not sacrifice; the saving and sanctifying work of the Holy Spirit) and the necessity of believing in Jesus (the Truth). Jesus does not permit other routes to God, whether continued Jewish ritual, Islam, polytheism, or a nebulous 'spiritualism'.

Jesus exposes evil deeds, so that only he who 'lives by the truth comes into the light, so that it may be seen plainly that what he has done has been done through God'.[43] A new covenant was being introduced, based on belief in Jesus as God and his salvific death and resurrection.

Whatever it is that we do, whatever forms of worship we use, if we do not accept Jesus as our Saviour and the only route to God, then we are not worshipping God. We have the form only, and not the reality. When we believe in Jesus, we believe in the truth, the Holy Spirit enters us, and we are given eternal life, and so we worship in truth and not mere form.

CONCLUSION

There are many good reasons for worshipping God which are worth meditating on, to help us in our Christian lives to love and want to worship God regardless of our surrounding circumstances. They lift up our eyes to heaven and the glory of God, and bring us comfort and assurance on earth. They remind us of the nature and character of God and inspire us to want to obey him and to put our trust in him. In this way worship links forward into obedience. And obedience also links backwards into worship: it is a form of worship, as our lives demonstrate God's character to others and bring glory to him.

CHAPTER 2

HOW WE WORSHIP GOD: BLASPHEMY AND IDOLATRY

I REMEMBER WHEN I visited a church in Zambia some years ago that the pastor asked us UK visitors a telling question: if your church left your area, would anyone even notice? It is a question that has always stuck with me because I am desperately afraid that for too many churches the simple answer is 'no'. No, no-one in the local community would notice. No, no-one would realise. No, no-one would care.

I think back to some of the churches that I have been to and consider which ones might trigger a reaction if they simply disappeared. There's the 'church on the hill'; famous on the local skyline and to all the truck drivers hauling their labouring vehicles up the long hill from the end of the Pennines before reaching the flatlands of Manchester. People would notice if that building disappeared, for sure. It was an established part of the local landscape, like the Woman's Institute or Brownies. The vicar spoke regularly in the local primary school, and people knew where to come for a wedding, christening or funeral.

Then there was the little church on the local council estate. We never had our own building, but we borrowed others'. We ran active kids and youth programmes, and we tried to help the adults in need. We never grew, but we tried; and I hope that people noticed when, after years of struggle, the church closed.

And then I think of a third church; a big evangelical church. Despite being based in a poor part of its city, it is very middle class. Apart from the students, I honestly don't know if many people outside of the congregation itself would notice if this church ceased to meet or moved elsewhere.

And finally there's a fourth church; a church I've only heard of from across the sea, from a friend who used to pastor there. This church inspires me and encourages me, and if you want to know what real Christian life looks like then I can recommend listening to their podcast.[44] This is the kind of church I think every church should be like. Here is what one of their members says:

'I went on a bike ride on Monday evening. I needed to get out of the house and convert my stress into energy, so that's what I did, and it was really cool. I thought I was going to do one of those cool guy things where I plug in headphones and listen to music and ride my bike by myself. But I actually ran into four guys on the bike path who go every Monday at the same time, and I had run into a couple of them once before, but I didn't remember their names. We ended up riding for about an hour together. And when you ride uphill on a bike, you ride pretty slow, so we got to talk because one of the guys was really slow. They asked me what I do… and I mentioned the Father's House – and they just spent the rest of the ride telling me about the Father's House; all the things they knew about it and all the great things, all the people they know. And they said things like, "Oh, my wife went to a women's group with some of the ladies at FHC, and she really liked it because they all talk nicely about their husbands." And then another guy said, "I knew about FHC because my workplace is always getting gifts for underprivileged kids for Christmas". I didn't have to say, "this is what I do"; they got to say, "this is what you guys do". They'd never been in the church… but I ended spending some good time with them and hearing the things they love about FHC.'[45]

Max had gone cycling, hoping for some peaceful time by himself, and instead ended up hearing from members of his local community, people whom he barely knew, just how important the church he attended was to them and the impact it made on their lives. These people didn't know God personally, let alone attend Max's church; they didn't even really know Max; but they knew of the Father's House Church and they could talk fluently about a church they'd never been in. The actions of that church brought glory to God's name.

How many churches can say that – that if you just mention its name to a stranger, they will be able to tell you all about what that church does for the poor and their neighbours? How many even know your church exists, let alone would notice if it closed? When your neighbours are in trouble, do they turn to you, or do they not even think of you? Does the young man, recently imprisoned, come to you because he remembers what you did for his family when he was a child? Does the addict come to you when he has nowhere else to turn and can't stay off drugs alone? Does the single mum come to you when she is tired and hungry, and her kids can't sleep for the cold, and she's just been sanctioned again because her bus was late for the jobcentre?

If people don't flock to us the way that they flocked to Jesus – not just because he had the words of life, but because he brought restoration and healing and justice – then maybe we're doing something wrong. Worse, maybe we're blaspheming God.

BLASPHEMY

The Bible is clear that we must not misuse God's name. This is not just about the words that we use, though blasphemy includes bad language about God.[46] There are also actions that can blaspheme God, including child sacrifice, theft, arrogance, sexual sin, injustice, false prophecy, idolatry, and teaching false doctrine. For example, the apostle Peter describes false teachers as blaspheming God's name by their 'destructive heresies, even denying the Sovereign Lord who bought them'.[47] They are people of sin, caught up in greed and 'lustful desires of the sinful human nature' (2:18).[48] Their lives and teaching are dishonouring to God.

As God's representatives on earth, how we behave affects what other people think of God. They expect us to reflect God's character in our behaviour, and thus when they look at Western Christians and see people who will twist the Bible to suit themselves, interpret the Bible in light of their own experiences and feelings rather than vice versa, and live selfish and oppressive lives, they will think that God – if he exists at all – is dishonest, selfish, and unworthy of worship. When we lead selfish, self-centred lives, we blaspheme God by making it look as though he does not care about poverty or injustice, or thinks the pursuit of self-interest is right and honourable.

God told the Israelites that 'anyone who sins defiantly, whether native-born or foreigner, blasphemes the Lord'.[49] Sin is dishonouring to God because disobedience shows a lack of concern for what God says, making it seem as though God does not matter to us. If the world sees Christians not taking God's word seriously, then the world will not take God or his word seriously either.

When God is merciful to us and does not judge our sin, it can appear as though God is weak and has no moral authority because he has let sinners and wicked people get away with wrongdoing. And when God is just and does punish sin amongst his people, it can look as though he is weak and unable to defend his people because they have been overwhelmed by pagan forces or natural disasters. Either way, sin brings dishonour to God by making him appear weak and unworthy – even when his mercy or his justice should be worshipped and glorified!

In Isaiah, God tells us that his name is blasphemed because Israel has been punished for disobeying God. God's necessary judgment on Israel meant that Israel became weak before the other nations, and those nations consequently mocked Israel's God as too weak and inefficacious to defend them.[50] Similarly, in Ezekiel, God's name is defamed because, 'it was said of them, 'these are God's people, and yet they had to leave his land''.[51] And earlier in Ezekiel, God explains, 'your ancestors blasphemed by not being faithful to me' and instead worshipped idols that they had made.[52] They were his people, yet they did not consider him worthy of obedience and loyalty.

Both through our disobedience and the penalty of our disobedience God is dishonoured. He is made to look small and weak, as though he is unable to protect us; our lack of commitment to him implies that he is not worthy of our commitment; and our sinful behaviour whilst we claim to follow God makes it look as though God also must behave badly.

In all these ways, doing wrong brings dishonour to God and undermines our other worship of him. Our sin is a blasphemy against God and blocks our proper worship of him.

IDOLATRY

John Calvin wrote of the second commandment that,

> 'As in the first commandment the Lord declares that he is one, and that besides him no gods must be either worshipped or imagined, so he here more plainly declares what his nature is, and what the kind of worship with which he is to be honoured, in order that we may not presume to form any carnal idea of him. The purport of the commandment, therefore, is, that he will not have his legitimate worship profaned by superstitious rites.'[53]

The first commandment tells us to have no other god before or besides the one true God. The second commandment says that we may not make idols and worship them. Although often read as merely forbidding the worship of other things, a point that is already made in the first commandment, John Calvin's wider interpretation is that this commandment relates not so much to whom or what we worship, but as to how we worship the one God.

Idolatry is, or at the very least includes, worshipping the true God in the wrong way.

This is serious. I doubt that many of us would imagine that we could be worshipping God in the wrong way. After all, how many ways are there to go about it? Surely so long as we're not constructing physical idols to call our gods, or killing animals or shedding blood, then we are not worshipping God wrongly? We're not like the Israelites who, after being brought out of Egypt by God, then got impatient waiting for his next word and so built themselves a golden calf to represent God and before which they could bow down – a behaviour they knew and understood, and assumed would be as appealing and acceptable to this God as it was to the various Egyptian and Canaanite deities with which they were familiar.

And yet God was furious.

The Israelites were doing what was normal to the local culture: make an image to represent a god, make offerings to it, and celebrate before it. That it was the real God they were trying to represent did not make it okay. God had forbidden that they worship him in such a way.

God cannot be tied to a specific form as if he is master of only one part of creation, such as the sun, the wind, or the animals. Nor can he be tied to a specific place, as though he is limited to a physical form with finite bounds. God is infinite, omnipresent, and creator – and therefore master – of everything. No physical thing can represent God and it is blasphemy to try; it is a dishonour to God to link him to his own creation and limit him in such a way.

Equally, we cannot interact with God in the way that pagan nations and tribes interact with their gods. The pagan gods had to be appeased or pleased through generous gifts and sacrifices, and then if they felt that the humans had given them what they wanted they might do something nice for the humans – or refrain from doing something nasty – in the expectation that such quid pro quo would encourage the humans to persist in bringing gifts and sacrifices. This was one of the reasons that the Greek gods loved Odysseus: for the sacrifices that he made them. But God cannot be appeased by us: our sin is too great. And he cannot be bought with gifts: there is nothing he needs that we can supply, given that he is the creator, sustainer, and owner of all.

The laws that God gave the Israelites were therefore not about creating a set of superstitious rites in which if the Israelites did X, then God would do Y. That would be to bring God down to human level and human interactions. The law had a number of purposes, but none of them were to reduce the relationship between man and God to the transactional relationship that pagans held with pagan gods. The law that God gave is much richer than that.

ISRAEL'S BEHAVIOUR

The Israelites of the Old Testament thought that they were good followers of Yahweh who obeyed the law that God had given them. After all, they had a host of commandments. They surely knew from the laws just what he wanted of them and didn't have to worry about not doing enough or not doing the right thing, for their God was clear in exactly what he wanted.

They had laws about burnt offerings, grain offerings, fellowship offerings, sin offerings, and guilt offerings. They had laws about how to remain 'clean'. There were animals they could not eat, and animals they could eat. There were skin diseases that wouldn't defile them, and skin diseases that would. There were regulations for purification

39

following menstruation, childbirth, semen emissions, and other discharges. There were laws about mildew and laws about avoiding the consumption of blood.

They had regular holy days on which they were to do no work. Every seventh day was the Sabbath day, which was a day for resting and gathering together in holiness before God. They celebrated their miraculous release from Egypt with unleavened bread and additional holy days. They celebrated the harvest by giving the first-fruits to God and by holding a holy day, a day of rest, 49 days after the day of the first fruit. They had holy days on the first, tenth and fifteenth to twenty-first days of the seventh month.

They came together in religious festivals and in fasts; they sang praise, sought God, and studied the Scriptures. They humbled themselves, asked God what his will was for them, and prayed for wisdom.

They were just like the Pharisees.

The Pharisees tithed everything, right down to their garden herbs, and they openly prayed and fasted for extended periods. They refused to defile God's holy Sabbath day by anything that could have even the semblance of work, even if that work was to help a person in distress. They honoured God so much that dedicating money to God was considered to absolve them of their duty to care for (elderly) parents. They praised God and brought him sacrifices. No-one was more dedicated to God and to honouring him than them.

Today, Christians continue the same practice of meeting together, usually on a Sunday. We tithe our income, make sure we're in our seat on Sunday morning, and attend mid-week Bible studies and monthly prayer gatherings. We look up to those who seem to pray more, study more, and turn up at church more. We want to be the people that always have something to share; always know where to find a verse in the Bible; can cross-reference with ease; and can pray flowingly for minutes at a time. We leave our families to go and spend time at Bible studies or prayer meetings.

We are just like the Israelites and the Pharisees.

But the Pharisees received some of Jesus' heaviest, most scornful criticism.

And the Israelites were condemned for their faithlessness.

For all that the Israelites and the Pharisees worshipped God, they worshipped him in the wrong way. And yet, they worshipped him in the way that he had laid down for them. So, what had gone wrong? And where do we do the same today?

BRINGING GLORY TO GOD

The apostle Paul exhorts us, 'in view of God's mercy, to offer your bodies as a living sacrifice, holy and pleasing to God'. He describes this as our 'true and proper worship'.[54] Furthermore, we are to honour God with our bodies, because we do not belong to ourselves but to God. He redeemed us from sin and Satan, and so we belong to him, and are to keep our bodies clean and undefiled, just as God is.

As well as worshipping God by refraining from doing wrong, we worship God when we do good things through his power and in his name. Jesus tells us that God 'is glorified by this, that you bear much fruit, and so prove to be my disciples'.[55] Jesus uses the metaphor of fruit to show whether a person is a true disciple or not. In this passage, bearing fruit only happens when we abide in God and he abides in us; this abiding only happens when we keep his commandments.[56] The implication is that 'fruit' in this passage is, or is dependent upon or associated with, the good deeds that Christians do in obedience to God. The fruit of obedience brings glory to God, just as disobedience brings dishonour to God.

Matthew records Jesus commanding us to 'let your light shine before men in such a way that they may see your good works and glorify your Father in heaven.[57] And Peter tells us to 'keep your behaviour excellent' so that those who observe us may in the end glorify God.[58] Paul says that those who claim to worship God should confirm this through their good deeds.[59] When we behave well and don't just refrain from bad deeds but actively carry out good deeds, then people take note. It glorifies God when people can attribute to him the good, not bad, behaviour of another person. It says that God is good too. We represent God to people, and how accurately we represent God matters.

John Piper explains, 'Since it is God's goal to be glorified in his people [Isaiah 43], and since Jesus says this happens when his people do good deeds [Matthew 5:16], we would expect the Bible to tell us that God's goal in redeeming a people is that they might do good deeds. And this is exactly what we find.'[60] In his letter to Titus, Paul says that Jesus 'gave himself for us to redeem us from all wickedness and to purify for himself a people that are his very own, eager to do what is good'.[61] Or, in a more readable format, 'He gave himself for us. By doing that, he set us free from all evil. He wanted to make us pure. He wanted us to be his very own people. He wanted us to long to do what is good' (NIrV).

God not only redeemed us in order to purify us to

do good deeds, but also created us in the first place to do good deeds. Paul writes that, 'we are God's workmanship, created in Christ Jesus for good deeds'.[62] Good deeds are therefore central to us both as God's creation and as his redeemed people. We are made and saved to be people who do good to others.

We know what is good both by what God does and what he commands in the Bible. In answer to a question about love, Jesus replied with a story about a man helping a member of a conflicting tribe who was in great need. There is little more sacrificial than this: going out of your way, and to substantial time and expense, to help a person whose only relation to you was that you were in the same place at the same time, and whose only claim on you was that he was in need. Jesus went one further: he deliberately went out to people in need – to us – when we were far away from him. He went to considerable time (33 years) and expense (giving up heaven and then his life) to people who had no claim on him at all: we were nowhere near him, and our need was entirely our own fault for rejecting him in the first place.

This love-action is what is good, and God wants us to be longing to do this and other good deeds. 'It is not so much by avoiding gross sins that God's people display his glory,' John Piper says, 'but rather in the pursuit of good deeds, acts of generosity, works of kindness, ways of love.'[63]

MORE THAN GOOD DEEDS

But it is not enough to merely do good deeds. The apostle Paul said that you can give all you have to the poor but if you do not have love then you are nothing.[64] Jesus himself said that whilst many will declare to him the good deeds they did in his name, he 'will tell them plainly, "I never knew you; depart from Me, you workers of lawlessness!'".[65] The most devout Muslim, Buddhist, or secular humanist is not giving glory to God through their good deeds. They do not attribute their motivation to the God who showered mercy and grace on us through his son Jesus. They do not find their strength to persevere in the overflowing love of God. Their love is not an outpouring of God's love. It is only when our motivation and sustenance is God's love that our actions result in glory to God.

For non-Christians, if their love is not based on God's love then their good actions are useless. For Christians, if our good actions are based on pride (like the Pharisees who wanted to look good before others) or legalism (obeying God in order to get to heaven, rather than in response to his love) then our good actions are useless. We can cast out demons in his name and call him Lord, yet never be known by Jesus. God cuts right into the heart of the matter, separating those who know him from those who don't, even when some of those who don't know him include people who think that they do. We cannot trust in our own good deeds, indicative as they are of the presence of salvation; we can trust only in God and Jesus' righteousness for salvation.

The apostle Peter says, 'Each of you should use whatever gift you have received to serve others, as faithful stewards of God's grace in its various forms. If anyone speaks, they should do so as one who speaks the very words of God. If anyone serves, they should do so with the strength God provides, so that in all things God may be praised through Jesus Christ'.[66] In all that we do, we are to do it to the glory of God[67] and with good will[68] and all our heart,[69] as people who work for the Lord, not for human masters. We don't merely do good deeds and incidentally bring honour to God; we do good deeds with the purpose and intention of bringing honour to God.

Whatever we do – whether speaking or serving or any other gift, whether in our working lives, family lives, church lives, or acts of charity – we are to do so as one who is sustained by God, so that God is glorified and not us. If our good deeds are to give God glory, then we must perform them as one who depends on God for resources and strength, for our entire ability and desire to do good deeds in the first place. We must do them as one who recognises God as Lord as well as Saviour, who willingly obeys him and recognises his command as what is good and true.

We are therefore to live lives that bring glory to God by recognising and admitting our dependence on him. We are to acknowledge that what we have and any success we achieve are through God and all praise therefore is due to him, not us. John Piper says, 'We owe every fibre of intelligence to God, and the slightest resolve to do good is a gift from him. Apart from him we are all cripples. And worse than cripples. We would fly into nothingness without his sustenance, and we would degenerate into devils without his grace. If the totality of our dependence on God would hit us full force, O, how differently we would live and do good.'[70]

AUTHENTICITY

Bringing glory to God requires that we honour his name through the holiness of our personal lives and the loving-kindness – the justice and generosity – of our public lives. It is as we obey the commands of God, not giving in to the pursuit of temporary pleasure but instead going out to love and serve others, that we bring glory and honour to

God's name. And when we do the opposite, then we are defaming God. To permit possessiveness, covetousness, and sexually inappropriate conduct in our lives is to defame God's name. When our characters do not match God's character and our lives do not obey his will, then we blaspheme against God. It is only when our characters match God's character, and our lives are obedient to his will, that we can truly worship God.

Shelby Abbott speaks about the loss of faith in many people who are brought up as Christians, reporting on the impact it has when God's people do not live up to God's character:

'It comes down to authenticity to what you're communicating from the pulpit or what you're communicating in youth group. And then, living the exact same way. I found that hypocrisy is not dealt with very well. People don't respond to hypocrisy very well. Even more so, exponentially more so today. If you're communicating something publicly, either from the pulpit or in the youth group, and your life does not reflect what you actually communicate from your sermons or your messages or your talks or whatever, people are quick to sniff that out... "What's the point? How's this [belief] going to work for me if the person who's supposed to be the professional Christian, the pastor... a person who spends their life preaching about it – it doesn't really work for them?" ... It needs to be intentional communication from up front about what the Bible actually communicates – so good theology that's communicated and how that's applicable to our lives – and then living it out as well, so that we don't

46

get certain things like hypocrisy, people walking away from the faith, hipster Christianity that's only popular because its mirroring what the world thinks is great… is there life change, communicated and then actually lived, with our leaders, I think that's a big factor.'[71]

Johnny Bowers, from the Father's House Church in Oroville, California, explained the same issue:

'The thing that used to bother me about Christianity before I was a Christian was that I didn't think that Christians were very genuine. I thought Christians were hypocritical. I'd have all these people that said they're Christians but they're partying right alongside me. If you want to be a Christian, then be a Christian. The word Christian means to be a little Christ, it means to be like Christ. That's a huge responsibility, that's a huge statement to say you're Christian.'[72]

Obedience to God is not about justification by works, but nor does our belief in justification by faith negate the requirement to obey God. The gospels are full of this, as some of the most explicit language about salvation is about actions: only the one who does the will of God will enter heaven;[73] the one who keeps God's word will never die;[74] the one who serves God will be honoured by God;[75] the one who hears and obeys God's word is secure in God;[76] it is those who obey as Abraham did that are the true children of Abraham;[77] whoever does the will of God is God's family.[78] Similarly, those who cling to the word and persevere will bear fruit,[79] and those who obey the word of God[80] and serve others[81] are blessed.

This is also phrased in the negative. He who does not obey God will be judged.[82] We must reject sin.[83] Whoever is not with Jesus is against him.[84] We cannot believe in Jesus whilst we continue to seek praise from other people instead of seeking the glory that comes from God.[85]

Jesus expects that his people will be able to obey him, because they will know what he wants from knowing and listening to his voice.[86] We are to 'see to it, then, that the light within you is not darkness'.[87] 'Whoever practices the truth comes into the Light, so that it may be seen clearly that what he has done has been accomplished in God'.[88] Everyone on the side of truth listens to Jesus.[89]

CONCLUSION

It matters how we live and whether our lives reflect God and bring glory to him, or deny him and blaspheme him. We need to live lives that match up to the teaching of the Bible and the character of God if we are truthfully to claim that we are his people. We need to be little images of Christ on earth, showing in our lives and actions what God is like and what he wants. If we don't, then all the rest of our worship – our songs, prayers, and Bible studies – are no better than idolatry. If we don't seek to obey God, then the worship that we do offer is no better than offering sacrifices to please false gods. Our lives become blasphemous when they do not match the character of God.

CHAPTER 3
GOD'S CITIZENS: FULFILLING GOD'S LAW

'THE HIGHEST DEGREE [OF charity] is to strengthen the hand of a Jew who is poor, giving that person a gift or loan or becoming a partner or finding a job for that person, to strengthen the person's hand, so that the person will not need to ask for assistance from others...

'A lesser degree, is one who gives Tzedakah to a poor person and is unaware of the recipient, who, in turn, is unaware of the giver. This is indeed a religious act achieved for its own sake. Of a similar character is one who contributes to a Tzedakah fund. One should not contribute to a Tzedakah fund unless he or she knows that the person in charge of the collections is trustworthy and wise and knows how to manage the money properly...

'The [third], lesser, degree is when the giver knows the recipient, but the recipient does not know the giver. The great sages used to go secretly and cast the money into the doorway of poor people. Something like this should be done, it being a noble virtue, if the Tzedakah administrators are not behaving properly.

'The [fourth], still lower, degree is when the recipient knows the giver, but the giver does not know the recipient. The great sages used to tie money in sheets which they threw behind their backs, and poor people would come and get it without being embarrassed.

'The [fifth], still lower degree is when the giver puts the Tzedakah money into the hands of poor people without being solicited.

'The [sixth], still lower degree is when he or she puts the money into the hands of a poor person after being solicited.

'The [seventh], still lower degree is when he or she gives the poor person less than he or she should, but does so cheerfully.

'The [eighth], still lower degree is when he or she gives the poor person grudgingly/with a feeling of pain/ unhappily.'

So said Rabbi Moshe ben Maimon in the Mishna Torah, Laws of Gifts to Poor People, 10:7-14. Rabbi ben Maimon was a twelfth-century Jew who was the first to index 'the entire body of Oral Law – both Talmuds, the various halachic Midrashim, later works authored by the Geonim, and even kabbalistic texts – and compile it all in a logical and systematic fashion'.[90] He also produced the 'golden ladder of charity' cited above, clearly showing how the provision of structural justice or opportunity far outranks the mere giving of money when it comes to charity or kindness to others. When some people talk of the cold hand of the state and the dignity of charity,[91] they would do well to consider that the argument may well be in the reverse: the supporting hand of the state, the dignity of justice, and the cold-heartedness of a person who thinks that money doled out at their whim can possibly be considered a just, let alone dignified, response to another person's poverty.

I can personally attest to the difference between charity and justice. I have a genetic chronic illness, hypermobility Ehlers-Danlos syndrome, coupled with Postural Tachycardia Syndrome and Fibromyalgia. The result is chronic pain, excessive need for sleep during the day, brain fog, and a wide range of other illness symptoms. Collectively it means I can't work enough to support myself, and depend upon the government for my income and for a contribution to the extra costs that I experience because of my illness. These costs include needing to pay for someone to cook, clean, tidy, wash up, and do laundry for me; mobility scooters and their maintenance; and taxis.

The UK government, however, has for many years taken the view that letting people like me receive an income from them is inappropriate. I should not, according to them, be dependent on the state. Rather, I should be out working. Fewer people like me should get state support at all, and the level of state support that the remaining people get should be reduced. This will give us a financial reason to get up, get better, and get out to work. Obviously, the only thing stopping us from work is not an incapacitating chronic illness but a bad attitude that uses a non-incapacitating illness as an excuse to be lazy.

My own experience, and the experience of my community, is that we have major illnesses that prevent us from engaging in as much activity as we would like. This is confirmed on a daily basis as, again and again, we are unable to fulfil our desires and meet even basic demands on our energy and health. Our daily lives confirm to us that we are unable to work enough to support ourselves, when so often we are unable even to engage in basic personal and household tasks despite not also being engaged in work. When we do engage in activity, the physical consequences to ourselves can be severe, and whilst this might be worth it for the gains in mental, emotional, and social wellbeing, that is not the same as being forced to engage in paid work under constraints determined by someone else.

Depending upon social security as I do has made the distinction between charity and justice very sharp to me. On occasion I have used a food pantry to secure food. A food pantry is a place that takes unwanted and otherwise waste food from supermarkets, restaurants, and other parts of the food industry, and sells them on at low cost to people in poverty. In the city where I live, there is no further room for food pantries or foodbanks, because all of the otherwise waste food has already been used up by the existing providers. But the demand remains high. Consequently, on around half of the occasions when I ask if I could buy a food bag that week, I am turned down. This 'charitable' provision of food is inadequate to meet the level of need.

The lack of supply is not the only problem with charity in general and this form of charity in particular. There is also a question of quality. The food I am given is usually on the edge of turning, if not already past its best. This means yellowing broccoli; bruised and mushy fruit; tough and stringy runner beans; vinegary fruit salad. It means food that doesn't keep, and ideally should all be eaten on the very day that it is given – and not all of it is suitable for home freezing. It means food that is losing nutritional value; food that has gone off; food that is no longer pleasant or enjoyable to eat. The items that have longer shelf lives are usually those that are highly processed and/or high in sugar. The overall nutrition balance is often 150-200% of RDA for fat and sugar.

Dignity remains a major problem. The food club that I use gives people bags of food rather than allowing users to select their own food. This feels deeply undignified as I am not even given the luxury of choosing what I eat, but am being told by someone unknown to me that I must have this food or go without. It means receiving high proportions of sugary food and ultra-processed food. It means getting a bag of food from which no coherent meal can be made. It means being given multiple items of the same thing, all of which need eating that day, rather than a variety of items and food that will last a week in the fridge. It means being given food that I dislike, to the point that I can't make myself eat it (especially when coupled with being past its best).

This charitable food is inadequate in quantity and quality to meet the need. It makes me feel like I am nothing more than a human dustbin for the middle-class, eating the food they don't want. By the time I have taken out the food that I can't eat (the sugary and processed stuff), the food that I really hate, and the food that is not really edible, I'm lucky if I've saved £5. And for that £5 saving, I'm eating food that I don't want; I've taken time out of my day to travel and to queue; I've made myself ill through the effort taken to go out and then when home to prep some of the food for freezing; and I still have to go to the shops to buy food to make up for the inadequacies of what I was given.

The food club that I use is not the only model available. There are other models that allow people to choose the food that they buy, and to queue indoors and in dignity rather than outside or in public places that lets everyone know you're the poor people come to eat the dregs of society. But the problem of insufficient food remains; and relying on waste food from the food industry will always create problems of unbalanced diets and excess amounts of food that has no remaining shelf life. But there certainly aren't enough middle-class people donating genuinely fresh food to meet the needs of poor and hungry people that way.

Contrast this with the income that I receive from government for being too sick to work. The money is my own, as of right; it is not subject to weekly variation based on the whims of charity or the waste of middle-class consumption styles. I can spend it as I choose, and thus to the best of my ability obtain a balanced and healthy diet. I have the dignity of choice, and I am not pointed out to random members of the public as one of 'the poor'. The only problem is that this income, too, is insufficient for a decent life – but the answer is to increase my access to justice, not to make me further dependent on the inadequacies of charity.

For Christians wanting to glorify God, we need to know what his approach to poverty is. Does he think poverty is something that is only addressed by rich people choosing to be charitable, or does he actually believe in organising society to have a structure that prevents and alleviates poverty? If we are to reflect God's character into the world and show the world how God thinks and acts, then we need to study the Bible to find out what God says about himself, about poverty, and about justice and charity.

But it is not good to simply cherry-pick individual verses, lifting them from the context in which they were placed and divorcing them from the narrative arc of the Bible. As others have pointed out, in the Old Testament Law there was no coherent separation between what we today often call moral, civil, or ceremonial law. For the Israelites, every law had to do with holiness. Every law had to do with God's character. We cannot, therefore, consider how we are to live and honour God by considering only some verses in isolation. We must consider the whole.

THE LAW IN THE TORAH
God and the Bible

The Bible is clear that God exists and is one God and the only God; that we must worship and not blaspheme him; and that we must obey him according to the words found in the Bible. When we worship God, we must do so in the ways that he has commanded – both in how we approach him and in the way that we live.

We are to love and fear God, learn and teach his word, not add to or take away from his word, pray to him, and worship him. God's word in the Scriptures is his revealed truth to us, not merely man's best efforts at understanding and approaching God. We must make sure that our lives, attitudes, and cultures are conformed to his word rather than attempting to conform the Bible to modern, secular culture. God also commanded the Israelites to listen to his prophets, and commanded the prophets not to prophesy falsely. For us, we can expect to need to listen to teachers who have walked with God and studied his word for longer than we have. And those teachers must take care to teach faithfully what God says. It is important that we do not distort the word of God, or we may lead ourselves and others astray, and fail to lead holy and God-honouring lives.

The Israelites had certain signs and symbols which they followed, such as circumcision and writing the Shema on a scroll and attaching the scroll to their doorways. These reminded them of God's faithfulness to them and the covenant that they were in with him. Christians have new signs, most particularly baptism and Holy Communion. We do well to use these opportunities to remind ourselves of the covenant that we have entered into with God, through Jesus' death on the cross and resurrection to glory.

Worship: Sabbath, Celebrations, Sacrifices, Cleanliness, and the Temple

By far the largest number of laws in the Old Testament are those that relate to the commands on how to ritually worship God. These are laws on things like sacrifices, cleansing and the difference between clean and unclean, festivals and fasts, sabbath days, and the temple. Whilst Old Testament scholars point out that the Israelites would not have seen the 'non-ritual' laws as distinct from the 'ritual' laws, as all laws were involved in the worship and honour of God, nevertheless there are certain laws that are more clearly related to those behaviours that are widely considered 'religious'. The point is not so much that there aren't at least some rough categories into which the different laws can be grouped, but that all of the laws had to do with the true worship of God.

But these laws are not guidelines for how to curry God's favour for whatever it is you want to do. They are not a series of steps for placating a capricious and sometimes unkind deity. Obedience to these laws does not confer upon a person the right to approach God or to make demands of God.

Instead, these laws tell us about God and our relationship to him. Cleanliness laws simultaneously kept Israelites clean from many public health diseases and kept them in a state of ritual cleanliness that reminded them of God's purity and inability to tolerate sin. The festival of unleavened bread reminded the Israelites of their dependence upon God their protector and deliverer, who rescued them from Egypt. The festival of first-fruits reminded them that God is their creator and sustainer, on whom they depend for food and life and wellbeing. The regular Sabbaths reminded them that their success does not depend upon their own efforts but upon God; and reminded them of the importance of having relationship with God. The Sabbaths also worked against the abuse and stigmatisation of labourers. It is hard to exploit the person who is celebrating alongside you at one of God's festivals, created equal with you by God.

So whilst these laws had a 'ritual' element, they also had practical elements. The Sabbath was a ritual holy day, and also a practical day of rest and a structural law against exploitation, and it was important enough that it happened weekly. Cleanliness laws maintained ritual purity, but also provided protection against spreading various infectious diseases and moulds to other people. These are things that we can reflect on as Christians: how even the more 'worship' focused of God's laws include measures for the protection of others. There is no sharp line dividing our worship of God from our treatment of other people.

The large majority of these laws cannot be kept today, due to the absence of the Temple and the inability to be ritually pure or offer sacrifices. But we can reflect on what each one tells us about God: about how he is our creator, provider, protector, and redeemer; about our position as created and fallen beings before him; about our dependence upon him and his worthiness of all our worship. The keeping of a Sabbath rest can be particularly valuable in a world that valorises 'hard work' and which seeks security in money, power, and one's own activity rather than in God.

Secular: dealings between people, employment, money, justice

Into this section I have put all of those laws which may be viewed as pertaining to morality. They may or may not also be 'legal' matters. Some of the 'religious' laws could also be put here, especially those pertaining to Sabbath rest (as this is one of the Ten Commandments); and also laws on cleanliness in so far as they prevented infected people, or infected objects, from spreading disease to other people and things.

More obviously, this section includes laws against things like lying, murder, theft, jealousy, coveting, anger, humiliating another person, and failing to protect a person who was in danger, as well as positive injunctions about loving and honouring others. Also included here are laws about setting up and running a fair justice system, and laws regarding the fair treatment of foreigners, employees (bond servants/slaves), and the impoverished.

Not all of these laws were encoded in Israel's justice system, in terms of having punishments attached to breaches of the law – though they all mattered in terms of breaching God's covenant and bringing his judgment. For us today, whether or not a given moral issue is carried over into a secular country's legal system often depends upon factors like the severity of harm caused by breaching the moral code; whether or not the secular world views that issue as immoral in the first place; and whether it may be deemed a private or public issue. For example, it is not in general illegal to lie but it is illegal to lie in a contract, lie on oath, or commit libel or slander. It is not illegal to break a promise between friends, but is illegal to break a business contract. These are issues where a moral question (lying or breaking a promise) only becomes a legal question when a certain severity or public threshold is crossed.

In other instances, issues which the Bible treats as immoral are not only not illegal, but may even be praised or valorised. It is not illegal to be greedy or covetous, and some economic schools of thought welcome these as drivers of economic growth, but they are immoral in God's eyes.

God's laws include some pre-emptive duties of care: putting fences around the tops of (flat) roofs;[92] not leaving dangerous items lying around;[93] rescuing a pursued person even at the cost of the life of the pursuer;[94] and taking action to ensure that an animal that has harmed a human does not have the opportunity to do so again.[95] There are also laws about helping those in need and looking after (honouring) one's parents. These laws place on us a burden to consider the protection and care of others. We cannot simply live as individuals as if our lives do not impact other people. These laws provide a principle for a duty of care which is seen today in regulations on the standards of goods and services, but which goes beyond these laws to include moral duties of care towards other people with whom we come into contact or who are affected by our actions and choices.

Personal relationships: sex and family

God gave quite a number of laws regarding marriage and sexual relationships. Most specifically, marriage is to be a monogamous relationship between a man and a woman, and the two must not be closely related by family ties. Marriage is not just a sexual act or a legal contract, but a reflection of the relationship between God and his people; between Jesus and the church. Sexual immorality is a sin against one's own body, and the body of a Christian is a temple of the Holy Spirit; therefore, sexual immorality is a sin against the temple of the Holy Spirit.[96] These laws therefore have a 'ritual' element to them, because of the sacredness of our bodies and our embodied state before God.

Many of these laws seem odd to modern Western thought, which does not see these sexual behaviours as immoral let alone something that should be illegal. Nevertheless, it is the command of God to us. It is something that the Bible say we must obey in order to honour and worship God. Still, this does not necessarily mean that these issues of morality should be issues of legality: sexual activity amongst consenting adults may well be an area that falls under the category of personal morality without being legislated on by government, just as many other moral issues are not legislated upon.

Other: rulers and wars

Although God did not want the Israelites to set up a king for themselves, he knew that they would one day want to and do so. He therefore pre-emptively gave them laws which forbade the Israelites from cursing a ruler or appointing a foreigner as ruler. He also forbade the king from accruing large amounts of wealth and property, including wives. God commands us to show respect to our leaders, and this is a moral law which continues today; but he also commands rulers to rule with humility and not to seek extra power and wealth over others.

In terms of the rules on war, these do not apply today as there is no theocratic nation acting as God's agent for justice. However, it is interesting to note that God's laws here were still concerned for welfare: a newly married man could not be asked to fight; and fruit trees were not to be cut down for war machinery. God's willingness to use nations to act as agents of justice against other nations also reminds us that all nations are called by God to adhere to certain levels of justice and right behaviour.

WORKING FOR JUSTICE
Worship

God gave the Israelites a lot of laws covering a range of areas, not all of which can be applied today. However, they can give us principles – they can tell us about God and about what God considers to be a good ordering of society. We need to study these laws and consider carefully what they tell us and how to apply them in any given context.

Some of the laws are more 'religious' than 'civil' or 'governmental'. This is particularly true around the issues of cleanliness, sacrifices, the temple system, and priests, Levites, and Nazirites. There is no-one today who can have ritual cleanliness, because the ritual purifications following certain sources of uncleanliness cannot be followed without priests and a temple. The maintenance of ritual purity for anyone has ceased to be possible. When we are unclean already, eating pork makes no difference to our state of cleanliness.

All Christians are declared clean from being washed in Jesus' blood. Most Christians interpret this to include the meaning that the laws on cleanliness no longer have to be followed, and so we are able to eat pork and so on. Similarly, there is no longer any need for sacrifices because of Jesus' death and resurrection as the final, ultimate, and complete sacrifice to which the earlier sacrificial system looked forward. These laws are carried forward neither into Christian's practical lives, nor into a country's legal system. But we do acknowledge them for what they tell us about God and our position before him. In that way, they continue to be true.

There isn't even any expectation or requirement that a country today be wholly Christian, which means that laws about blasphemy and the worship of God remain true for Christians but are not part of a country's legal system. Christians are called by God to honour him and glorify his name, but this is not a matter for secular law other than for governments to permit freedom of religion and belief. Christians should desire to obey God, and to study his word in order that we may know how to obey him, but that does not mean that we impose this requirement upon non-Christians. We should love God with all our heart, soul, mind, and strength and love other people as God has loved us; and love our enemies too – but such love cannot be enforced by secular law.

Secular law

The Bible gives us a strong moral code, but it doesn't follow that every moral issue should be a legal issue. Aquinas argued that law cannot prohibit all vices, for this would bring the law into contempt through the inability of any human to keep it. Instead, 'human law prohibits only the more serious kinds of vice, from which most persons can abstain, and especially those vices that inflict harm on others, without the prohibition of which human society could not be preserved.'[97] At the same time, 'The behaviours which law or policy promote and discourage, impose and forbid, help to shape what society holds up as worthy of moral praise or blame, as morally virtuous or vicious'.[98] These are all things to think about when we are considering which moral issues should be encoded in law.

Indeed, not all of the laws given by God came with a punishment for breaking them. They were, if you like, written into the religious or moral law, but not into state law. It should not seem odd to us, therefore, as Christians to see that some issues which we consider immoral are not illegal in our country. Matthew Martens writes, 'For some moral wrongs, the sword of the state is a disproportionate response... Many wrongs can and should be addressed in much less serious ways to ensure the response is proportional to the offense.'[99]

God clearly cares about justice and right behaviour. He gave the Israelites laws that protected property, safeguarded lives, and administered punishment. He instructed them in the creation of a judicial system and the right behaviour for those who act as judges. But he did not require that every moral issue be a legal one. Wisdom, therefore, is needed when reflecting on how God's laws for the Israelites are to be implemented in practice today.

One of the issues for Christians to reflect upon when voting is which of God's principles belong to state law and which do not, even if a whole country agrees that it is immoral. It may be immoral to lie, for example, but it is only against the law when it occurs in certain situations such as a legal contract or when giving testimony in court. Or a government may choose to recognise some legal contracts such as marriage, and therefore have laws regarding what is and isn't a marriage, and how a marriage is legally dissolved, but that is not the same as legislating on what is sexually permitted. This does not mean that sexual behaviour ceases to be a moral issue for Christians, but simply that there is no state punishment for most sexual activity between consenting adults.

For Christians, this can cause difficulty when there

is not only disagreement over whether a particular moral law should also be encoded in a legal system, but whether it is a moral issue at all. Many Christians, for example, consider abortion to be murder and therefore should be illegal, and this has also been the historical Christian position; yet for many non-religious people and some more liberal Christians, abortion is nothing more than a question of a woman's body, healthcare, and right to choose. The developing baby is assumed to not be a person and therefore not be something – someone – that could be murdered. Or on the question of sexual interaction, same-sex intercourse is so far from being seen as immoral that it is increasingly seen as something that it would be immoral for society to forbid. It not only should not be illegal in state law, but should be positively made legal through the legal acceptance of same-sex marriage contracts.

These differences between what modern secular society views as moral, and what traditional or historical Christian positions have held to be moral, can be challenging. Thinking about what it is reasonable to ask non-Christians to abstain from, and what history shows it is practical to ask people to abstain from, may be helpful for Christians on this matter.

Justice

Justice is not just about the criminal justice system. It is also about the systems that work to prevent or promote (socio-economically) just outcomes. It's not just about whether one individual hurts another, and whether such an act is punished by a regulating authority. It is also about whether the systems and structures in a society routinely block one group of people from accessing a good to which they need access to live and thrive, whilst another group or groups have access. It wouldn't make sense, for example, to say that it is 'unjust' for someone to go hungry when there is a famine and everyone else is equally hungry; but it is unjust if some people have more than enough food whilst others can't get enough because of forces outside their control.

When we vote, we need – in the interests of justice – to consider whether the person or party we vote for intends to enact policies that help or harm the poor. If someone is proposing a policy that appears to cause immediate direct harm (such as cutting benefits or reducing spending on health and social care) then we should think very carefully before deciding to help enable such policies. If I want to support a party that intends to make work-search more punitive for unemployed people but will lower taxes on the middle and upper classes, then I need to be very sure that a lack of punishment for unemployed people is a major contributor to poverty and unemployment in this country. We should strive to find out whether these policies do bring the indirect good that they are alleged to bring, and what is the collateral damage. We should equally scrutinise policies that seem to promote a direct good, for the risk of indirect harm or inadvertent collateral damage. We should also consider who has the most responsibility to act and who has the most ability or can act in the fairest or most efficacious manner.

Oliver O'Donovan argues that government should act in those instances where, if it were not to act, some injustice or public wrong would occur.[100] Augustine said that, without justice, nations are just large-scale bands of robbers. It takes the desire to act justly to separate a government from a robber.[101] So justice is about whether those with less access to money and power can get what they need. It's about whether poor people can afford to access the justice system or whether the rich win because they can afford a better defence team. It's about the rights of the poor, needy, and vulnerable against those with wealth, health, and power. If governments are not interested in this, then they are just bands of robbers.

There are a range of ways in which we can measure the justice of a society. We can consider whether everyone in the country has what they need to not just survive but to also do well and have the opportunity to contribute to family, community, and country. The Centre for Research in Social Policy at Loughborough University caries out research on this every year, to establish the minimum income that a given person or household needs in order to not be excluded from society. In 2020/21, 29 per cent of working-age adults in the UK were living on less money than is needed to have an acceptable level of social inclusion.[102] This figure is worse for children, with 40 per cent or 5.1 million living in households that did not have enough money to participate fully.

We can also consider access to legal justice: can people get fair representation in court, or does the person with the biggest pockets win more often than a just consideration of the law would suggest? Can people get timely access to a trial – whether as defendant or plaintiff – or are they left waiting months, or even years, whilst evidence erodes, and witness memory becomes less reliable? Are people left bankrupt by a trial – again whether as defendant or as plaintiff, and regardless of where the 'truth' lies – or are costs spread so that those who have borne the emotional and cognitive burdens of a trial are not further penalised through financial loss as well? And when a guilty verdict is found, is the punishment proportionate to the crime;

and can the person re-enter society fully after serving the punishment or do they continue to suffer extra-judicial harm beyond what is just and proportionate?

Writing towards the end of 2023, trial dates were being set for the end of 2025. Between 2009 and 2018, the police lost 22,000 officers, and budgets (other than for counter-terrorism) fell by 20 per cent between 2010 and 2015.[103] Meanwhile the Crown Prosecution Service saw its budget cut by 30 per cent between 2010 and 2019, and lost a third of its staff.[104] The number of court and tribunal judges fell by 12 per cent from 2012-2022, whilst magistrate numbers fell by almost a half.[105] Legal aid – payment for barristers for people who otherwise cannot afford to access justice – has been so cut-back that it is virtually non-existent, forcing 'people and their families [to] endure adversity which affects their health, work, accommodation and social relations.'[106] Junior criminal barristers in their first two years earned less than £13,000 pre-tax in 2019/20 whilst working 70 hour weeks,[107] regularly going unpaid for work that could keep you or a loved one free from prison for a crime that you didn't commit.

Social mobility is another indicator of the fairness or systemic justice within a society: whether people genuinely get equal opportunity to succeed and thrive, or whether people living in poverty do not get the opportunities that other people have. It is not just or fair for your ability to thrive to be determined by where and to whom you were born. One of the potential roles for the government of a given country, therefore, is to help to even out the unfairness of life caused by birth and fortune; to reduce the role that luck – and in particular, being born to rich parents – has in one's quality of life.

Social mobility in the UK is low. This means that if you

are born poor, chances are you will stay poor: the 'sticky floor'. Equally, if you are born rich, then chances are that you will stay rich: the 'sticky ceiling'. For every 20 children born to parents in professional jobs, 12 enter professional jobs themselves whilst only 3 enter working class jobs. For children born to working class parents, 7 in 20 would enter professional jobs and 7 would enter working class jobs – but they would earn less in those jobs than the child born to a professional parent. The apparent mobility in profession for working class children is countered by a continued depressed impact on their income. 'Ultimately,' says the Social Mobility Commission, 'class plays an outsized role in a person's ability to move up the income and jobs ladder, and there has been no measurable improvement in recent years.' [108]

The changes in inequality and social mobility over the past decades show clearly that government policies have an impact on the fairness of a society. The Nordic countries, with their relatively high levels of state investment and low levels of inequality, also have high social mobility. It is entirely possible to do much better than the UK currently does in ensuring that everyone has opportunity for a decent life.

CONCLUSION

Societies have choices; and governments have a role in, and responsibility for, creating structural and economic justice. When Christians vote, therefore, we should be considering which policies are most likely to advance such justice. We should think carefully about which moral issues should be regulated by government, and which fall to individual decision; which areas the government should regulate and act to modify, and which should be left to individual freedom. When we are weighing up which party or individual to vote for, we need to consider how our vote directly and indirectly impacts upon other people. We may be helped in this by thinking about what God, in the Bible, has revealed to us about the principles and goals of a fair society, and in particular the role of government and structural justice.

CHAPTER 4
GOD'S SOCIETY: AMASSING WEALTH

JACK SAT QUIETLY IN THE consulting room, staring forlornly ahead at the single marshmallow squatting humbly on the plate before him. He made no move to eat it, but sat quite still. The seconds ticked by. The child's hands twitched; he pulled them away and determinedly shoved them behind his back. Moments later, he rose and moved swiftly to the corner of the room, where he crouched and pushed his knuckles into his eyes, humming to himself as he did so.

The seconds continued to tick by. The boy, tired of his corner, got up and began to pace back and forth along the short wall, darting glances at the marshmallow as he did so. Finally, unable to resist any longer, he sprang to the table and, grabbing the marshmallow, stuffed it into his mouth.

Like most other young children, he could not wait 15 minutes to earn a better treat. Chances are that his life as an adolescent and adult will be less successful than if he had been able to hold out the full 15 minutes.

This 'marshmallow test' was carried out over the late 1960s and early 1970s; 550 largely middle-class children of 3-6 years old participated in the experiment.[109] The basic experiment was to leave the young child in a room with a small treat, such as a single marshmallow, and tell them that if they could wait until the researcher came back before eating it, then they could have a bigger treat as well. There were some variations, such as whether the smaller treat was visible during the waiting period or not, but the broad approach remained the same. In general, the children could not wait the full 15 minutes, but the length of time for which children were able to wait was correlated with abilities in later life such as exam results.

The authors of one of the early follow-up papers cautioned that the causal mechanism between the ability to wait longer for a treat and success as an adolescent or adult had not been established. However, they posited that 'the qualities that underlie effective self-imposed delay in preschool may be crucial ingredients of an expanded construct of 'intelligent social behaviour'. Over time, this and other studies following the same children[110] became the source of an urban myth that children from poorer backgrounds do worse as adults because they have some sort of character weakness, as seen in their lesser self-control as children. It was used as an explanation of why such children do worse as adults and why it is their own fault.

And yet, the very same paper recognised that the decision to wait for a better treat depends in part upon the surety or otherwise of that better treat being forthcoming. 'In a given situation, therefore, postponing gratification may or may not be a wise or adaptive choice.' In a situation where, say, the researcher has already proved that they don't follow up on promises, then it is not a wise or adaptive choice to wait for the better treat. Chances are that it will not be forthcoming, and to delay eating the available, lower-value treat has no benefit. The correct adaptive response would be to eat the treat whilst it was available, rather than risk losing it in the vain hope of being given something better.

This is what later studies examined in more detail. Yes, children who waited longer before eating the less desirable treat – and the handful who waited the full 15 minutes – did perform better as adults. But was this because they were better people, or was it because they had grown up in environments where delays in self-gratification were rewarded from a young age? Was it because this was an adaptive learned behaviour, which happened to set them up well for adult life? For children who waited less time, or the few that did not wait at all, was it because they were of weaker character, or was it because the environment that they had grown up in was one in which, if you didn't take the available treat now, the likelihood was that you would end up with no treat at all; whilst the likelihood of actually receiving the better treat in return for waiting for it was low? The real issue may be that children from poorer backgrounds grow up in environments in which the best adapted behaviour is not well suited to middle-class definitions of success in adolescent or adult life, which require a different learned behaviour.

Later studies found that the link between waiting for a treat and adult achievement was small, and was reduced even further after controlling for family background, early cognitive ability, and the home environment.[111] Perhaps more importantly, the decision to wait longer for a better treat was related to the trust that the child had in the researcher's reliability[112] or in people more generally.[113] This is important, because children from poorer backgrounds may be more likely to experience unreliability: parents who can only promise to buy a birthday present if they get the shifts that week to have the money, or buy a Christmas present if the weather is mild so the heating doesn't need to be on, or buy new shoes if the washing machine doesn't break down again, or attend their child's football match if they aren't called in for a shift at the wrong time. When your early childhood is spent learning that perseverance doesn't pay off, and that quiet behaviour earns no reward, and that delaying gratification means losing it completely, then the set of behaviours that you learn in order to succeed in your world are not the behaviours that achieve success in the middle-class adult world. They may, however, continue to be the behaviours that achieve the most liveable lifestyle in the world that middle-class adults have picked for you: the world of low-pay, insecure, variable hour, long shift, dead-end jobs with no skill beyond your ability to work fast for long hours at a time, no matter how tired or ill or sore you are. And when, having adapted to this world, you are unable to work your way out of poverty no matter how hard you work or how long your hours, you will then be blamed for your poverty because of your 'bad character'. Yet no-one ever gave you a world in which middle-class attitudes and behaviours towards life would have paid off.

This is one aspect of inequality and how it causes harm. People living on lower incomes are not simply living in the same world as middle-class people, just with less money to spend. They are not living in small but well-insulated, draught-proof yet ventilated houses in areas with tree-lined streets, plenty of parking, good public transport, good local schools and doctors, and lovely public parks or fields and hills. No, they are living in cramped housing with limited insulation, probably ill-fitting single-glazed windows, and major problems with cold, damp, and mould; on a crowded street; where the public transport is intermittent and insufficient; the schools and GP surgeries are poor, as all the best teachers and doctors seek pleasanter areas where the pay is higher and the workload substantially lower; and access to real nature is next to none. And the jobs market? Good luck finding anything that won't make you ill through the physical overload and the mental and physical toll that this takes; good luck finding anything which is secure, let alone offers a career progression; good luck finding something that has regular hours let alone something that co-ordinates well with public transport so that you're not waiting – or walking – hours at two in the morning because the next bus doesn't come until 6am.

Take four children, two who at 22 months old are in the top 10% and two who are in the bottom 10%. At age ten, have these children remained in the same relative positions? No: their performance at age ten depends not so much on their performance at 22 months as on the incomes of their parents. The two children born into the richest families are the two who perform best at age 10, even if one of them was in the bottom 10% at 22 months. And the two children who were born into the poorest families are in the bottom 10% at age ten, even though one of them was in the top 10% at age 22 months. That's inequality. And it affects these children for the rest of their lives.

GOD'S SOCIETY: ISRAELITE SOCIETY IN THEORY

In Israel, every person had an inalienable right to land and home. However poor a person became, however lowly, they were to be fully restored in the year of Jubilee, which came round every 50 years. They would not just be set free, but would also be put in possession of what they needed to live: a home and a means of livelihood. In an agrarian society as Israel was, land was everything. It was both your home and your source of income. Being unable to lose your land permanently was a big deal. It meant that everyone could start again. Everyone had security. No-one could be permanently deprived. At the same time, if someone was poor, the system meant that they were provided with the minimum needs for dignity, by working as servants under good working conditions and kind masters who took responsibility for their wellbeing.

Those who had not fallen so far and had merely accrued debt, without the loss of land, had that debt cancelled every seventh year. If they had reached the point of needing to sell themselves into service, then that was also cancelled in the seventh year. During years of service, the master was expected to provide for his servant; at the seventh year, the servant was restored to working for himself again. In case those with money would be unwilling to lend to people in the sixth year, when repayment was less likely to be achieved before the year of debt cancellation, God expressly forbade this as a wicked approach to take.

God's concern was not with the rights of those with money; it was with the needs of those without. He placed a strong duty upon not just the nuclear family but the extended family and the whole nation of Israel to provide for the poor and protect those who were undefended. There was simply no way out of helping those in need without breaking God's law. If you were family, you helped. If you had money, you helped. You didn't help in a way that made money, in the manner of pay-day loans, renting out your surplus property for profit, or selling necessities for profit. You helped in a way that increased the prosperity of the other person *whatever the cost to yourself*. If you had the money to redeem a relative or lend to a needy man then you did so, even if it was nearly the seventh year. And when it was time to let your debt-servant go, you sent him away with a golden farewell.

The flip side to protection against poverty is pre-emption of wealth. In God's economy, the only income you could legitimately receive was the real merit of your own hands, and that is inherently limited. You could not exploit the poor by paying them less than their work was worth, exploiting their need for any money at all and skimming off the profit to yourself. You could not lend with interest and so nor could you make money out of lending. You could not purchase extra land indefinitely, creating a monopoly or super-control that forced people into paying you money for the privilege of access to land that was given to them by God. And if you ever did end up with more money, then you merely had greater responsibility to care for the poor.

In God's economy, if you lent to someone and wanted to be sure of getting it back, you would have to work with that person to get them to a position where they could repay you before the seventh year. Lending wasn't an economic transaction with the overall aim for the lender of making money; it was a creation of a relationship to the benefit of the borrower. You lent in order to help, and making money wasn't even a side-benefit; it simply wasn't allowed. You ended up neutral or in negative territory as the lender, and that was right, because like with the collection of manna when the Israelites were in the desert, no-one needs to have any more, nor should have any less, than they need.

From an employer's perspective, there was no such thing as increasing profits by driving down wages and working conditions. Employment wasn't something you went into to make money, but to give money. You looked after all your employees, you were responsible for their welfare, and you paid them a more-than-liveable wage. You didn't think about how to amass your own wealth; you thought about how to look after your employees and produce quality goods. You even let your employees go with a generous gift: not the golden good-byes of retirement, but a golden 'fare-well in your new business and life', which business may well compete with yours. 'Love your neighbour' applies even more when that neighbour is also your labourer, and therefore under your power and your responsibility; it still applies when that neighbour may be about, with your help, to become your competitor.

ISRAELITE SOCIETY IN PRACTICE

In theory, there would have been no poor people in the land of Israel, and nor would anyone have grown rich at the expense of others, so inequality would be low. But the history of Israel is that God had to repeatedly send prophets to call his people back to him – even when his people had no idea that they were far from him. Archaeological evidence shows that, whilst initially there was income and wealth equality within Israel, this did not last. The Israelite society became unequal; a situation which God had forbidden, and which could only occur by neglecting the laws on economic and social systems.

The Israelites failed to keep the economic and social laws that God gave them, even as they thought that their obedience to the sacrificial and cleanliness laws kept them righteous before God. This neglect of God's laws outside of their religious lives meant that they were very far from God. Their unawareness of their sin should act as a dreadful warning to us of the power that money and worldly things can have on us.

WEALTHY PLANS

God's commands to the Israelites would have prevented both poverty and riches. Unfortunately, the Israelites neglected these economic and social laws, and they were even unaware that they had sinned by not following God's laws in these areas. The prophets therefore were sent by God to challenge his people, showing them their sin so that they could recognise and repent of it.

Micah speaks woe to a people whom he describes as 'devising iniquity' and 'plotting evil' even in their beds. This iniquity and evil is the iniquity and evil of planning to accrue more wealth to oneself. Plotting even in their own beds showed just how deeply engrained this attitude was in the plotters' lives. The whole bent of their lives was towards themselves, their own gain, and money. These are people who judge for a bribe, teach for a price, and tell fortunes for money – yet do so in ways that they have excused to themselves as acceptable.[114] They can be as small as the grocer tipping his scales ever-so slightly in his favour,[115] or as typical as a ruler taking gifts, or those in business working together to favour their own aims,[116] but God likens all such deceit, theft, and exploitation to murder and even cannibalism.[117]

In Jeremiah 22, God calls out the wealthy. The summary of God's judgment against the wealthy is that they have not administered justice nor rescued the oppressed from the thief, and instead they have done violence and wrong to those who are unprotected and killed those who are innocent. This strong language does not necessarily refer to leaders who literally order the deaths of their citizens; after all, this is a group of people who broadly think that they are faithful to God. Rather, the strength of the language reflects the strength of God's feeling against any failure to protect and provide for the poor, let alone against those who are active agents of harm in stealing, failing to pay correct wages, cheating people in business transactions, and so on.

This is not merely an Old Testament principle for a theocratic nation. James is just as stark in his language, telling the rich that they should 'weep and wail because of the misery that is coming' upon them for the sin of hoarding money.[118] We more easily remember James saying that the wages which the rich have failed to pay their workers cries out against them, but that is not James' only charge. He also challenges them for living in luxury and self-indulgence.[119]

Jesus gives us a parable to make the same point. In Luke 12:13-21, Jesus tells a story of a landowner whose land produces a bumper crop. Delighted, the man immediately considers how he is to best live in the future now that he has so much. He decides that he will pull down his existing barns and build bigger ones to store his crop, and then he will live off the proceeds of his crop for many years. But God says to him, 'You fool! This very night your life will be demanded from you. Then who will get what you have prepared for yourself?'.

The point of Jesus' parable is the wrong attitude of the man towards wealth. We know this, because Jesus tells the parable in response to a man asking of him, 'Teacher, tell my brother to divide the inheritance with me.' Jesus says that he is no judge or arbiter – although indeed we know that God is the source of all justice, and justice would have been to divide the inheritance as laid out. Instead, Jesus tells the crowd, 'Watch out! Be on your guard against all kinds of greed; life does not consist in an abundance of possessions.' Then he goes into this parable.

Jesus does not say in this passage how much of the landowner's bumper crop was due to the landowner's personal effort. Perhaps it was all his work; perhaps he deserved all the reward – although that is unlikely. It would be physically impossible that a single man could bring in all of such a large harvest by himself, let alone then build a barn in time to store it all. He must have employed labourers. Did he give them a bonus in line with the bumper crop that year? Did he consider how their work had contributed to what he clearly thought of as his crop? There must have been good weather; as any farmer knows, it is so easy for a lack of rain at the right time or too much at the wrong time to damage the crop. Clearly there was no locust swarm that year. Did the farmer give a higher proportion – not just a higher absolute amount, but a higher percentage of the already higher total – of the crop to God in thanks to His goodness?

Perhaps he did give his labourers a bonus and did give an extra part to God. But he still kept the majority back for himself so that he could cease to work. And so there is a deeper point than how much of the bumper crop was due to the landowner's personal effort, and how much was due to others' work or to chance events.

The landowner's response to the crop should not have been affected by the extent to which he deserved it, or felt that he deserved it, or felt that others did or didn't deserve it. His response should not have centred on himself, on how he could bless himself and what good this crop could do for him, regardless of the extent of his merit. He very likely over-estimated his merit, but even if he were right, he still should not have seen that as a reason to keep it to himself. His response should have been to joyfully consider how he could best use this crop to bless others. Yet all he thought about was himself. Everything was about not having to work in the future, and devoting his future time to his own pleasure, with no thought about the plight of people who were in need now.

Chances are that the landowner did not merit all the profit from the crop, but that he thought he did. This is a major fault to which we are all prone. In a rigged experiment, researchers brought in pairs of participants to play a game of monopoly.[120] Based on a coin toss, one player would play as normal, and the other would start with twice as much money, collect twice as much when they reached the Go square, and move round the board twice as fast by rolling two dice each turn. As the game went on, the rich player placed their pieces more loudly; displayed signs of dominance and power; became ruder and less sensitive to the poorer player; ate more of the provided snacks – and finished up by citing their own skill and game choices as key to why they won. The researchers report that, 'They became far less attuned to all the different features of the situation – including that flip of the coin – that had randomly gotten them into that privileged position in the first place... [it]'s a really incredible insight into how the mind makes sense of advantage.'

As wealth increases, feelings of compassion and empathy go down, and feelings of entitlement and self-interest go up. Richer people are more likely to justify and moralise greed as a good behaviour, and self-interest as favourable and moral.[121] Richer people are less likely to help other people. When rich and poor people were brought into an experiment and given $10, then told they may share it with a stranger, poorer people gave 44% more than did richer people – despite needing the additional money more. Richer people are more likely to cheat in order to win, and to steal what is dedicated to others (in this case, sweets that they were told were dedicated to children in a developmental study). Rich people are also more likely to illegally fail to stop for a pedestrian at a zebra crossing: in a study, the drivers of the 20% cheapest cars all stopped, yet close to 50% of drivers of the most expensive cars did not stop. Richer people are more likely to endorse unethical behaviour such as taking cash from a cash register, taking bribes, lying to customers, and lying in negotiations. Given the ethics of the rich, it becomes unsurprising that they are so suspicious of the poor and assume high rates of cheating and gaming the social security system – yet they are wrong to do so, for the poor are far more ethical than them, and are not only less likely to cheat but also more likely to help others who are in need.

Greed is a very pernicious sin. It is one of which we are so easily unaware. There are a great many reasons and excuses we can come up with to justify our own behaviour and perhaps, very occasionally, some of them are right. But by and large they are not.

It is never right to pay less than a living wage, even if your argument is that it is better for a person to be paid some wage than not be employed at all. That is only an excuse to allow consumers to under-pay for what they buy, or for business owners or shareholders to extract profit to which they have not contributed, or even for unproductive or unprofitable businesses to exploit cheap labour. It is never right to employ people in working conditions that may make them ill, even if you pay a living wage for the privilege of being able to exploit them in a different way. If you are taking on an intern, you are on very shaky ground if you claim you do not need to pay them for their work because they are paid adequately in the experience gained, as if people could feed themselves off their CV. If you are taking on a volunteer, you should consider carefully how you expect your volunteer to live, and what use is made of their work – certainly it should never be to your own or a shareholder's profit. Indeed, if you're a profit-making company rather than a community-interest company or charity, you should not be using volunteers.

If you feel your excuses jumping in and your hackles rising – then I can only humbly submit that you haven't realised the strength and severity of God's commands to us that we not only pay the labourer his due but help the poor in his time of need.

SEEKING GOD'S KINGDOM

Following the parable of the foolish landowner, the gospel writer Luke goes on to Jesus' sayings on worry, God's kingdom, and the treasure of our heart. Here Jesus extends the Old Testament teaching that we are not to hoard possessions to ourselves but instead use what we have to defend and provide for others. Now God says that not only are we not to make plans for how to make wealth, but that we are not even to make plans for how to get the necessities of life. Jesus says that we are not to seek, search for, require, or demand (*zēteite*, Luke 12:29 'be concerned for') what we will eat and drink, and nor are we to worry about what we will wear.

Instead, the seeking that we are to do is for the kingdom of God. It is the same word, *zēteite*, in Luke 12:29

as in 12:31 where we are to seek the kingdom of God. The effort that the secular world puts into seeking money and possessions and position and power, we should put into pursuing God's kingdom. Indeed, the effort that we ourselves so easily put into pursuing the necessities of life we should put instead into pursuing God's kingdom. Jesus reassures us that we are not to be afraid of doing this, for God knows what we need and is pleased to give us the Kingdom.

Where the foolish landowner stored up riches for himself that would not last and could not be kept, we are to store up riches in heaven by selling our possessions on earth in order to give to the poor. But note that the virtue is not in selling our possessions. It is not in living an ascetic life. There is no minimum amount of possessions which bestows upon a person an extra holiness or godliness. God, after all, is rich in everything that is good. He is not an ascetic. Rather, the virtue is in giving to the poor. It is in having the heart of God, which is to give to others.

THE TREASURE OF THE HEART

We do not always realise where the bent of our thoughts and our heart lies. Jeremiah tells us that the heart is deceitful above else, and only God can search and know it.[122] This is why it is so important that we take the time to think deeply about what the Bible has to say and how that applies to our lives. It is far too easy to be as the Israelites were, and to so excuse our sinful behaviour as to be utterly unaware that it is sinful, and that we are sinning.

The verses we have seen so far have been clear that wealth is typically a sinful position, usually because it has been acquired by sinful means but at the least because it means a failure to give out that wealth to people in need.

And yet most Christians in the western world live middle-class lives in middle-class houses with all the middle-class expenditure that that entails.

Where have we gone so wrong? We do live in a culture that is unusually individualistic and pro-wealth. The economic and social system in which we live is one that praises income and wealth inequality as a positive force for getting the poor to work harder. We grow up in a culture that believes the best thing for everyone to do is to seek their own personal good. But the problem does not seem to me to be uniquely western. It is not our western culture that makes us so individualistic, but our natal individualism that makes our western culture what it is. The Israelites started with the best economic system that there is, at least for an agrarian community without advanced technology, and yet they distorted and corrupted and changed it in the same ways that westerners live today. The problem of individualism, self-centred living, and money-seeking behaviour is universal to all people, in all places, at all times.

The problem is in our heart. Our hearts deceive us as to our own actions. Of course, they are our own hearts, and we have responsibility for them – we cannot blame our sin on our hearts as though it is not our fault that we are deceived. We have the Bible ready to shine its light into our lives and root out all sin if we are prepared to listen. We need to be prepared to scrutinise our hearts, whilst also not trusting what they tell us.

Jesus tells us that the question is where our heart lies. Does our heart lie with money and earthly treasure? Or does it lie in heaven with heavenly treasure? The foolish landowner was a fool because he stored up treasure on earth instead of in heaven. He should not have worried about how to find food or water or clothing, let alone about storing up luxury. He should have been rich towards God, which is achieved by selling possessions – or not buying them in the first place – in order to give to the poor. When we sell in order to give to those in need, we convert our earthly possessions into heavenly treasure. The extent to which we do this reveals to us where our hearts lie: on earth with earthly things, or in heaven with God.

We should be very wary of the threat that money poses to our lives. Agur wrote in Proverbs 30:8-9, 'give me neither poverty nor riches, but give me only my daily bread. Otherwise, I may have too much and disown you and say, "Who is the Lord?". Even Solomon, the wisest man on earth, oppressed his own people and worshipped false gods. His great wisdom could not protect him from wealth. If you don't give money away for the sake of the poor, at least do so for your own sake lest you become entrapped by it.

Jesus tells us another parable to emphasise this point in Luke 16:1-13. There was, he said, a dishonest manager who was found out and about to be sacked by his employer. Shrewdly, he considers to himself how he can best lay-up provision for his future life. He knows that what he needs is people who will welcome him when he is poor and powerless. So he goes to his employer's debtors, and for each one cancels a large proportion of their debt, thus winning their favour. Jesus says this to make the point that whilst we are on earth we should make a friend of God, winning his favour for our future poor and powerless state when we die. By using 'worldly wealth' or the 'wealth of unrighteousness' – the things of earth – to provide for those in need, we store up favour in heaven, which is where, ultimately, we need it.

This is a complex and nuanced parable, that certainly is not meant as an endorsement of deceitful behaviour. Nor is it saying that we are saved by how we use wealth on earth. Jesus' point is the attitude and approach of the man: using wealth now to improve his future lot. So, too, should we use the wealth we have on earth in a way that stores up treasure for us in heaven. Jesus uses this example as a kind of satirical critique: if even selfish, corrupt people can use money wisely to store up favour, can you Christians really not use worldly wealth in a way that will store up treasure for you in heaven? How terrible to be out-performed by the world on this!

OWNERSHIP

Jesus makes a further point in Luke 16: that the wealth we are called to use to help the poor is not even ours in the first place. And, he says, if we cannot be trusted to use other people's (i.e., God's) wealth to help the poor, who will trust us to handle our own wealth properly? If we are not faithful in the use of God's possessions, he will not give us our own in heaven.[123]

As God repeatedly pointed out to the Israelites, there was nothing they could give him that he did not already own. God is the creator, sustainer, and therefore owner of everything: every animal of the forest; the cattle on a thousand hills; every bird in the mountains; every insect in the field; the day and night, sun and moon, summer and winter; the heavens and the highest heavens and starry hosts; the silver and the gold.[124] All that is, belongs to him.

When God gave the Israelites the land of Canaan, it did not become their possession as a matter of absolute, or allodial, right. God told the Israelites, in regard to the law of redemption of land every 50th year, that, 'The land must not be sold permanently, because the land is mine and you reside in my land as foreigners and strangers'.[125] God retains the ultimate ownership, which means that his laws apply everywhere in the world, and everyone owes him certain dues. One of these is to use his possessions for the good and blessing of others.

The things of the earth do not belong to us, because we are not their creator. But they also do not belong to us because we are sinners. We not only have no right to claim ownership, but we have even forfeited the right to tenant-ship and stewardship. As sinners we forfeited the right even to govern God's possessions. We have no God-given inherent right to the ownership of whatever is in our possession, but hold it in trust for him, to use wisely on his behalf.

God entrusts us with his possessions, for the heart of God is not for gathering all things under one person, even if that person is himself, but for sharing so that others can enjoy his good creation. He delights in sharing. He is also a God who particularly provides for and protects the poor. If we are truly followers of God, then our hearts should reflect his.

The things of this world are given to us for our blessing, but God's blessings are not things to be grasped. God says that when we give to others, then he gives to us: a good measure, shaken and pressed down and running over.[126] There is no need for God's people to hold tightly to what they have, fearful of losing it. Instead, the more we give the more we receive from him. It is a scary thing to do, but those who have given the most to others on behalf of God report a joy and closeness to God that cannot be achieved any other way. When we hold on so tightly to the things of this earth, we miss the much greater things of heaven that God offers. We are truly like the child of C. S. Lewis's depiction, so fearful of losing our mud pies that we reject the sand and the sea of the beach.

THE HARM OF INEQUALITY

The god of wealth is also the god of injustice. The two are either side of the same coin. Jesus says that we cannot serve both God and money, and nor can we worship God truly if we continue to pursue wealth, keep wealth to ourselves, and fail to enact generosity and justice for the poor. We need to link our economic, public lives with our private and 'religious' lives. Too often we live like the Pharisees, and fail to secure justice for others; we outwardly appear to be good, up-standing citizens, but our handling of wealth reveals us to be internally filthy hypocrites.

Christians should know not to pursue wealth or valorise inequality, because the Bible tells us this; yet for forty years that has been the key economic model of the UK and much of the world. It has been the particular economic model of the economically right-wing Conservative Party, but has also been incorporated into the left-of-Conservatives (but still often right-of-centre) Labour Party. Many of our leading economists and politicians actively praise inequality for the benefits they believe it brings. Boris Johnson, for example, said in 2013 that 'some measure of inequality is essential for the spirit of envy and keeping up with the Joneses that is, like greed, a valuable spur to economic activity.'[127]

It is ironic that in the USA, as far back as 1995, some 85% of people said that they placed a high value on responsibility, family life, and friendship; yet 95% also thought that 'most' of their fellow Americans were (unlike them) materialistic in their outlook.[128] If everyone thinks that way, who is it that genuinely supports the consumerism of modern Western societies? We all live sufficiently consumerist lives that people looking at us think we're consumerist – and we all think that we don't want society to be that way. And in the UK, 75-80 per cent of people have over the past two decades consistently believed that income inequality is too high, despite underestimating the level of inequality – yet still we have a society that supports, enables, and even welcomes inequality.

Economic harm

The policies enacted by a government are based upon its understanding of economy and society. A flawed understanding of economics, society, or individual behaviour results in flawed policy that at best doesn't help, and instead frequently harms, the people whom the policy makers want to support. If a government believes that inequality is a positive force, then it will enact policies that enable and even encourage inequality. If it is thought that inequality is profoundly negative, then a completely different set of policies will be utilised – ones that seek to actively help people at the bottom, rather than help people at the top; ones that curtail high levels of wealth rather than cut support for the poor; ones that understand that equality of opportunity is about costly investment in poor areas, not giving the poor less in order to 'create' a 'work ethic' that they ostensibly don't have (and, coincidentally, letting rich people off the hook for taking action).

For economists, this is an empirical question: what impact does income and wealth inequality have on the economy overall and poor people in particular? For Christians, inequality is a moral question which the Bible clearly indicates is wrong and which should never have been accepted. Just as Christians always argued that the universe had a beginning, even though science did not agree until the twentieth century, so Christians should not have accepted the arguments of economists that inequality, greed, and envy are positive features of an economy, society, or individual life. It is interesting that studies show that inequality is harmful for everyone, but it shouldn't have taken research to convince Christians of this truth. We have God's word. Nevertheless, we now have empirical evidence too, and perhaps that will help convince those of us who still cling to the neoliberal mantras of promoting greed and inequality – a belief that is not just wrong but harmful; and not just harmful for the poor, but harmful for the rich too.

The International Monetary Fund, a body that has previously strongly advocated for austerity as a response to recession (a typical neoliberal position), has since come out confirming that more income and wealth equality is better for the economy: recessions happen more often in more unequal countries; and greater equality is associated with better and more durable economic growth over the longer term.[129] Inequality is associated with boom and bust cycles which temporarily look good – creating political pressure on those governments which are not growing their country's GDP as fast as those captured by the neoliberal mythology – but result in bigger and more frequent busts which, over the long-term, mean a smaller economy compared to more equal countries. During the busts – recessions or depressions – neoliberal economics advocates further cutting by central government, but this merely exacerbates and prolongs the economic difficulties by cutting total demand in the economy even further. In the UK, economic growth from 1990-2010 would have been more than 20 per cent higher (going from 40 per cent to 50 per cent) if inequality had not risen between 1985 and 2005.[130]

Using tax and social security to redistribute income and reduce income inequality does not harm economic growth. This means that there is no reason to fear such distributive policies. Not only that, but it isn't only the very poorest who are helped by such policies. Everyone benefits from a more equal country. And improving incomes of people in the 11-40 per cent range boosts the economy, just as increasing incomes in the bottom 10 per cent does.

One of the arguments for neoliberalism and income inequality was that this would result in a bigger economy and greater income and wealth for poor people, even as the very richest ended up with an even bigger proportion as well as absolute amount. But instead, neoliberalism has both reduced the size of the economy relative to a more equal country, and has reduced the share of that economy which is available to poor people. It has done the opposite of what was promised.

In the East Asian 'miracle' economies, strong economies are founded on common traits that include 'promoting economic development by explicitly favouring certain sectors; commanding competent bureaucracies; placing robust, competent public institutions at the centre of development strategies; clearly articulating social and economic goals; and deriving political legitimacy from their record in development.'[131] In the Nordic countries with their high social cohesion, health, and wellbeing, success comes from 'universal social policies rather than reliance on targeted, means-tested selective policies; reducing poverty through welfare state redistribution policies; relatively narrow income inequalities; emphasis on equality of opportunities *and* outcomes according to class and gender, and for socially excluded groups; a broad scope of public services with provision of services mainly by the public service at local level; social spending and social protection...; [and] no one single policy solution but an accumulation of policies across the life course, each with its specific effects.'[132] There are a variety of specific policies and policy mixes which can vary from country to country, according to its specific needs and industries, but the successful countries share common features of a commitment to the common good and a rejection of neoliberal and free-market positions.

Political and social harm

Inequality does not just harm the economy. It harms the political and social sphere too.

Having more money means you have more power, influence, and control. This enables you to get even more money. The business owner wins in the argument over pay, working conditions, and regularity of hours not because she is right but because she has more power. When the worker wants to take the business owner to court, he can't because he hasn't got the cash, and the government got rid of Legal Aid that used to help poorer people access justice. And then the worker finds that what the business did isn't even illegal because the government watered down protections for workers. And the government did this because the business owner lobbied them, claiming that her business – and therefore the country – would suffer if the government didn't favour the business owners over the workers.

When rich people buy political favour, poor people start to lose faith in the democratic process. Rich people have the government's ear; poor people give up even trying to talk. Governments may then lose legitimacy as 'loser's consent' is withdrawn if people feel that the wealthy bought the election or the policies that are implemented. Poorer people and disempowered people may start to feel that protest – even disruptive, dangerous, or violent protest – is the only way to get their voice heard; or that in a world where the rules don't seem to apply to the rich, then they might as well disregard the rules too.

Inequality divides people. Most people choose their friends from those in a similar social position to them. If society is sharply unequal, then fewer people fall into the 'people like me' band, and there are many more people either below or above us. These 'other' people are rarely met and interacted with – creating, at best, uncertainties about who they are and what they are like; and, more often, a degree of suspicion, distrust, and prejudice. This may have relatively little impact when a poor person mistrusts the rich; but when the rich mistrust the poor, their outsized influence on the political sphere encourages and enables policies that are downright harmful to the poor. The rich may even genuinely believe that what they are doing and advocating is good for the poor, but their social separation keeps them ignorant of the reality both of what policy is actually needed, and what their policy is doing.

People have no objection to differences in income that are earned: it is accepted that doctors merit a higher salary than cleaners, vital as both jobs are, because the doctor required years of specialised training as well as practice under supervision, whereas cleaning well is predominantly about repetitive practice and does not require a university degree. What people do object to is unearned differences: raising one's own pay by driving down pay for underlings, over-charging customers, and not paying for harm to the environment; or making money merely by having money rather than by work. These sorts of unearned, extractive, exploitative, and rent-seeking behaviours are unjust. The injustice is made even more pernicious when it is considered how much political and legal power this money buys.

If your own hard work doesn't receive a just reward, whilst other people's inherited wealth and extractive, exploitative behaviours continue to earn them huge rewards, then the basis for society is undermined. There is no trust that you can build your way to a better life, or that those who hold huge power deserve and therefore can be trusted with that power. There is no trust that the government will do what is good for you and yours, rather than for the richest and most powerful. There is no trust that you will get justice in any dispute between you and those above you in the income scale. There is no faith that we are 'all in it together' rather than each just out for his- or her- self. There is no confidence in paying taxes towards societal goods or universal services; no belief from the rich that they will get anything back, or the poor that they will get anything at all. All of this badly undermines confidence in the political system and in the fairness of society. The result is that inequality correlates negatively with social cohesion and trust.[133]

Governments in unequal countries often spend large amounts of money on 'welfare' and public services – like prison. They are spending in response to problems that are caused by or substantially related to inequality. A government could spend less money for far better outcomes in health, education, housing, social care, social work, police, and criminal justice if it only sought first to enact policies that support greater equality. Instead, pandering to the reluctance of the rich to spend money on helping the poor avoid negative outcomes, they end up spending far more on the individual and social consequences of these negative outcomes and their impacts across the whole of society. Captured by the self-interest and short-sighted desires of the rich to keep their wealth to themselves, governments fail almost everyone.

There is no way of allowing inequalities of income and wealth without also having inequalities of power and inordinate influence over society. Yet this is the opposite of the Christian way. Our God is not one who seeks more power or glory to himself, but one who deliberately empties himself of power and glory in order to serve others – and undeserving others at that. Christians should be emptying themselves of power and glory, not seeking more of it. And we should challenge governments to take the same approach – for politicians to empty themselves of their high view of themselves and what they deserve, and instead to focus on building up the poorest and least powerful in society. This is, after all, why we have 'ministers' and 'prime ministers' rather than emperors and lords.

Individual harm

Inequality is harmful to individuals, even those at the very top of the scale. For anyone below the very top, it is harmful because of the inequalities in access that it creates and damage to physical and mental health. For any inequalities of opportunity to be acceptable in society, therefore, they must not be too big, and they must not derive from any unfair or unmerited means.

Richard Wilkinson and Kate Pickett's 2009 book, *The Spirit Level*, documents data on multiple health and social issues that correlate with inequality both globally and between USA states. Greater income and wealth equality in a country is associated with improved figures on physical health, mental health, obesity, child wellbeing, teenage pregnancies, drug abuse, violence, imprisonment, education, social mobility, and trust and community life.[134] Wilkinson and Pickett explain how 'health disparities are not simply a contrast between the ill-health of the poor and the better health of everybody else. Instead they run right across society so that even the reasonably well-off have shorter lives than the very rich. Likewise, the benefits of greater equality spread across society, improving health for everyone – not just those at the bottom. In other words, at almost any level of income, it's better to live in a more equal place.'[135]

It can even be better to be poorer in a more equal country than richer in a less equal country: rates of diabetes, hypertension, cancer, and heart disease are all higher in the top third of USA citizens than in the bottom third of UK citizens.[136] But that doesn't mean the UK can relax: death rates of the poorest people in Sweden are lower than for the richest people in UK. On these measures, it is better to be poor in the UK than wealthy in the US, and better to be poor in Sweden than rich in either the UK or US.[137] Even for children of well-educated parents, being in a more equal country means you yourself are likely to achieve a better education. For children of less well-educated parents, the difference is even bigger.[138]

This is not due to cultural differences. Culturally similar Portugal and Spain have different health, wellbeing, and social outcomes that are correlated with their respective levels of inequality. Culturally very different, Japan and Sweden both perform very well; both have low levels of inequality. Nor is it to do with government spending: many highly unequal countries spend large amounts on 'welfare', because the cost of reacting to inequality is greater than the cost of providing equality of opportunity, access, and participation.

'Being at the wrong end of inequality is disempowering', says Michael Marmot, 'it deprives people of control over their lives. Their health is damaged as a result. And the effect is graded – the greater the disadvantage the worse the health.'[139] There is a classic UK dataset that makes this point beautifully. It is the Whitehall Study, and its first finding, using data from 1978-1984, was that health and longevity improves as one moves up the civil service ladder.[140] The civil service is not a low-end job; even at the bottom, these are jobs of reasonable quality compared to the real bottom of the labour market. Nevertheless, lower civil servants had a mortality rate four times higher than those at the top, and mortality fell as one moved up the hierarchy.

Gradients in smoking, obesity, and blood pressure were too small to explain the finding. The important factor is control: the amount of control you have over your job. People higher up the career ladder had jobs with greater responsibility – and they also had more control over the work that they did. That made the difference. In contrast, people in low-status jobs didn't have that flexibility and personal control that people in higher jobs had. This is true not just in the civil service, but across all types of work.

The kind of work that exists at the bottom of the pay scale – where the emphasis is on speed of performance; there is very little variation in job task; and even what hours you work are not under your own control but the employer's random beck and call – is toxic.[141] These 'high strain' jobs put a lot of pressure on people's bodies and minds, without a commensurate level of control, and that is what makes them so sickening. Sir Michael Marmot described one such warehouse job as though the employer had 'taken everything we know about damaging aspects of work, concentrated them in a syringe and injected them' into their employees.[142] 'Inequities in power, money and resources are the fundamental causes of inequities in health'[143] – and the greater the level of inequality in a society, the larger these inequities.

Being of higher or lower status in a hierarchy has negative impacts on a person's physiology, even if they have the same material resources. This is shown in animals that naturally form hierarchical groups, such as macaque monkeys. If a selection of high-status macaques are taken from their existing groups and put together, then some of those macaques will (by necessity) become low-status in the new group. These macaques suffer from a rapid gain in atherosclerosis of the arteries.[144] These animals can't be blamed for their condition; they are quite capable of being top-ranked macaques. It is an inevitable consequence of the social stress of being lower down the pecking order.

In humans, a similar effect is seen in developed countries where a higher level of inequality is associated with increases in stress-related conditions such as obesity and heart-disease for people at the bottom of the income scale.[145] It is not that these people want to be ill or have chosen ill-health. The social situation in which they have been placed materially impacts their physiology in ways that are outside of their control – but are in the gift of wealthier individuals, who have more political influence and can lobby politicians to build a more, not less, equal society.

There seems to be an assumption that ongoing economic growth is an axiomatic good. And yet, once past

99

a relatively low point, economic size no longer correlates with health and wellbeing of a society and its citizens.[146] The USA has a national income per citizen double that of Greece, but its life expectancy is lower. Japan is between the two for income and has substantially better life expectancy than both. If Greece wants to improve its outcomes on a wide range of health, wellbeing, and societal measures then it need not pursue greater wealth but should pursue greater equality. If we want the UK to be a better country and society, then what we should pursue is not more wealth – which we do not need and will not help our outcomes – but greater equality of income and wealth.

The World Economic Forum writes that, 'most economies are failing to provide the conditions in which their citizens can thrive, often by a large margin. As a result, an individual's opportunities in life remain tethered to their socio-economic status at birth, entrenching historical inequalities ... most countries underperform in four areas: fair wages, social protection, working conditions and lifelong learning.'[147] The UK doesn't make it into their top 20 countries for social mobility. Countries that do well are those which 'combine access, quality and equity in education, while also providing work opportunities and good working conditions, alongside quality social protection and inclusive institutions.'

When there is low social mobility, a country tends to split geographically between poor and rich areas. An original intention for social housing was that, having been awarded a social house for life, a family could improve their income and remain in the same house. This would mean that over time there would be a mix of people of different income levels in the same neighbourhood. This principle has been lost as social housing was sold off and not replaced, with the result that social housing is now in such short supply that it is not always possible to allow families who have increased their income to remain in a low-rent property. Consequently, these people lose their tenancy, and move out of the area whilst other, poorer people move in. Those who move out have to leave their home, and also often their local family, school, and networks. Those who move in may not have these social supports, resulting in an atomisation of society instead of the strong community that we know to be a positive and desirable feature.

When a neighbourhood is comprised predominantly of poor people, then a 'ghetto' effect occurs such that poverty isn't about a person who happens to have a low income whilst living in an otherwise decent area with good access to nature, clean air, education, healthcare, jobs, and so on; but instead is about poor people living in deprived areas and lacking the means to compensate for the lower quality of the place where they live. There is a vast difference between a low income in an area with good public services, a pleasant environment, and neighbours earning above the minimum income standard compared to living in cramped, poorly insulated housing in an area where there are few jobs, few opportunities, poor education, poor healthcare, and a poor living environment. This geographical separation itself then helps to contribute to poor social mobility, creating a vicious cycle that can only be overcome by investment and a commitment to decent public services and equality of opportunity for everyone. Crucially, this includes building houses that are set aside for the poor – because otherwise this investment into poor areas just sees these areas taken over by the better-off, and the poor are pushed out to another deprived place.

Summary of inequality

Income and wealth inequality is multiply bad for a country. It actively harms the economy, by undermining and destabilising economic growth, and by sucking wealth up to the top, where large amounts become static (i.e., they are saved rather than spent) and are effectively removed from the economy compared to money that is in the hands of the poor. It harms society by creating imbalances of power which in turn lead to imbalances in access to politicians and policy makers, which leads to decisions that favour the rich over the poor and undermine social cohesion and trust. It harms almost everyone by reducing the control that those below the top 1% have over their lives, which harms their health and wellbeing, and has knock-on consequences for the whole of life. It harms the poorest people by pricing them out of access to decent jobs, housing, healthcare, education, justice, nature, and more. And inequality even harms the rich, by damaging social cohesion and increasing the overall levels of violence and criminality in a country.

If cutting support was the way to get people out of poverty (the assumption being that they then enter jobs), we would have seen it happen over the last 40 years. But it hasn't happened, and instead every piece of data that we have says that it is supporting people – giving them more, more accessible, better quality, and more timely help – that makes the difference.

Wealth at the top has not helped the poor at the bottom, yet its doing so was the only moral justification that such levels of personal wealth ever had. What makes the difference to poverty is government policy: pensioner and child poverty fell when governments increased financial support to these groups; and child and working-age adult poverty rose again when governments cut support to these groups. Michael Marmot writes, 'if societies want to *increase* inequalities of income and wealth, then they should do the following: transfer publicly owned assets into private hands; be complicit in low general rates of income growth, but engineer the economy so there are runaway salaries at the top, make taxes on income and spending less progressive; reduce taxes on capital, including corporation tax, capital gains and inheritance tax.'[148] It sounds very familiar. It is no surprise that we suffer from inequalities of health, power, and opportunity when these are the policies that we vote for. Yet none of this is necessary. Justice demands that we do not permit it.

CONCLUSION

Christians should not have needed economic and social research to tell us that we should help people. We should not have needed the secular world to tell us that grace and mercy are central to success. We should not need left-wing politicians to tell us that creating structural justice is a key role of the government. And yet, time and again, we have failed to challenge the secular world on its economics of injustice and inequality which has perpetrated great economic and social harm across not just the UK but the whole globe.

The church does not exist to assuage the conscience of political leaders. It exists to bring God's kingdom into being on earth; to act as a demonstrator and proclaimer of the ethics of God's kingdom; to be a representative of God and show his character to the world. When governments make choices that clearly – or even potentially – harm poor people, the church should say so. Leaders of the church are responsible for not leading their people astray;

for not proclaiming peace when there is exploitation; for not saying that God is with us when we are not with him. If church leaders do not want to speak directly to government, at the very least they should speak to their congregations about what oppression and exploitation looks like today. Citizens of God's kingdom should know and respond to what their government is doing, and seek to ensure that they themselves do not engage in exploitation or oppression of the poor.

CHAPTER 5
GOD'S PEOPLE: THE RICH PATRIARCHS

I AM A REASONABLY KEEN gardener and love to be out in the sun, on my knees tending to my flowers and vegetables: removing weeds; adding compost; trimming overgrowth; collecting seeds. Some of my plants seem to thrive with minimal attention; others have taken a few years to get established but are starting to grow strongly; some have, sadly, died – most likely due to a lack of care and attention from myself.

One plant that doesn't need any help at all to thrive is horsetail. Horsetail is a pernicious plant, a relic from before the time of the dinosaurs, which spreads everywhere and is incredibly difficult to get rid of. It sends roots out underground ready to pop up wherever it can find a route to the light. It can't realistically be dug up, because the roots are widespread and will go as deep as two metres, and a fragment of root left accidentally in the soil can generate a new plant. You could put weedkiller on it, but you have to abrade the surface first so that the weedkiller gets through the tough skin, and you're at risk of killing adjacent plants and not getting enough on to kill the horsetail. It can only really be stopped from taking over a garden by pulling up the stems whenever they are seen, and by checking for it repeatedly and thoroughly; and this has to be done forever. You also need to actively cultivate good plants that you do want to crowd out the space for the horsetail. Even then the horsetail hasn't gone; it's just not competing successfully with the other plants anymore when it is being specifically targeted. If any neighbour has horsetail in their garden, it will cross over into yours, constantly regenerating the pool of horsetail in your garden.

This is what money is like. It creeps into every part of our life. It grows deep in our hearts and pops up in unexpected places. It is almost impossible to eradicate and requires constant vigilance. We can never relax around money.

Money is deeply attractive and deceitful; so much so, that we can barely afford to have any, lest it deceive us and lead us away from God. At best, it causes us to harm others both materially by not helping and spiritually by blaspheming God to these people; at worst, we also lose our salvation. This is, after all, the God who said that it is harder for the rich to enter heaven than for a camel to pass through the eye of a needle; and who declared that those who are saved are those who feed the hungry, give water to the thirsty, clothe the naked, and house the homeless.

Even for those who have regularly given away their wealth and sold out of pension funds, money is still a trap and a danger, as Steve Orsillo says:

'Money and sex, the pride of life, the fear of failure – those kinds of things are probably the most powerful … you can say you're free from the love of money, but you've got to be on guard all the time because of how seductive is. I've lost so much money, and I have had so much money... but just like that, a snap of your fingers, and I'll have a hundred dollars and know somebody needs it and I'll put it away so nobody can ask me for it; so if they ask me, I don't have it [with me]. Then I get convicted, and put it back in my pocket, and say 'Lord, you're free to have them ask me.' But there for a minute, just for a second, I got caught up in putting my wallet away so that if they ask me, I can say I don't have it on me. And I catch myself playing that game and realise ... if you're not willing to let go of $10 or $100 then you're really not free from money.'[149]

Generosity has to come before wealth. Steve tells of a young man who said he wanted to be a millionaire, so that he could do good things. So, Steve asked him, 'Are you doing good things now?' And the guy replies, 'Well, I only have a little money.' 'Yes, but with that money are you doing the little things that that money can do? Are you giving people ten dollars who need ten dollars?' And he said, 'no, but when I get the money, I will.' Steve replied, 'if you won't give the ten dollars when you have ten dollars, you're never going to give money when you have a million dollars. The intoxication, the disease that is going to come upon you, is going to overwhelm you. This money will destroy you. If you're not giving from your small amounts, from your need, there is never enough money... money is a powerful, powerful force that can really hook you.'[150]

In another podcast, Steve says, 'If you know of a ten dollar need today, and you're not meeting the ten dollar need out of your need – you can't afford to meet it, but you're doing it out of faith – then when you have a million dollars or a bazillion dollars you won't be meeting some ministry's needs. You'll feel the pull of that money and you will be unable [to give] if you don't practice giving from need. If you have a dollar and someone asks for a quarter, that's a lot. And if you're not giving from the quarter, if you're not giving from your need, more than you can afford, when you have a little, you're not going to give more than you can afford when you're rich. Rich people never have enough.'[151]

I can't recall hearing many sermons that speak of wealth as an injustice, or that didn't start a sermon on money or giving with 'there's nothing wrong with being wealthy'. It feels like every time the Bible discusses wealth in a negative light, or generosity in a positive light, the first thing that's said is that it's okay to be rich and keep our riches. In one sermon I heard on the parable of the soils, the speaker went out of his way to say that 'the deceitfulness of wealth' did not mean that it was problematic to pursue a nice house for yourself. I worry that the speaker was himself deceived by wealth if he could say such a thing.

In my experience, teachers seem to be at pains to stress that it's not about how much wealth, savings, and assets you have, but about your attitude towards what you do or don't have. The emphasis seems to be on saying that the issue isn't about financial riches or poverty, or physical, material abundance or lack, but about our heart attitude towards money and our concern for those who don't know God. It feels as though, every time a sermon is preached on wealth, the teacher is weakening the message by 'spiritualising' it.

In the Sermon on the Mount, Jesus takes clear physical laws – murder and adultery – and, far from weakening them, instead strengthens them by spiritualising them.

Contemptuous anger against another person is the spiritual equivalent of murder. Looking at a person lustfully is the spiritual equivalent of adultery. If a person demands something of you, give them double. When you meet someone who is opposed to you, even slanders and discredits and oppresses you, treat them as a friend. What would it look like to strengthen the command to give to the poor by spiritualising it?

One argument that Bonhoeffer makes in his book *The Cost of Discipleship* is that it is only those who have come through the other side – who have given up all their wealth and physical possessions and blessings for God – who can really hold their possessions 'lightly', having them as though they did not, and having the right attitude towards God and possessions. And in the parable of the Good Samaritan, the Samaritan does not merely give up his money. He also gives up his time, his effort, his energy, his care – even perhaps his reputation, by being hours late for wherever he was going. He put concern and compassion into making a relationship between himself and the injured man, even though the injured man was a stranger, an enemy and, as far as he knew from a distance, potentially a fraud.

It is rare, and very difficult, to have wealth and yet not have a wrong heart attitude towards God and wealth. But it is not impossible.

THE RICH PATRIARCHS

We know that a number of major people in the Bible were rich. Typical examples are Job, Abraham, David, Solomon, the women who supported Jesus and the early church, and the people reported in Acts as giving money to the church (at least up until the point that they gave it!).

But we need to be careful not to read into simple statements of fact what we want to hear. The Law permitted divorce, but Jesus said that this was only because of the hardness of people's hearts. Many men in the Old Testament times had multiple wives, yet the Church holds polygamy to be against God's ways. Abraham, Isaac, Jacob, David, and Solomon all engaged in unethical behaviour that we are very much not meant to emulate. The fact therefore that followers of God have historically existed with wealth does not mean that God condoned their wealth or condones wealth in a Christian. We need to consider carefully what the Bible does and doesn't say, as well as taking care not to read Western understandings of wealth into Israelite society.

Some of these key Old Testament characters acted as 'types' of Jesus – their lives foreshadowed some of what Jesus would come to do on earth both the first and second time. Joseph is one such type, who because of his betrayal by his brothers ended up in a position of authority where he could do much good through dispensing food to those in need. He was showered with wealth by the Pharaoh. David and Solomon, in their position as kings, represented the future rule of Jesus. As such, their wealth, position, and power symbolise the wealth and prosperity that will be here when God restores all things to their natural order before him, rather than wealth that we can expect to have on earth now before Jesus' second coming.

The Old Testament patriarchs also lived in a different covenant with God, in which Israel as a nation would be blessed if she obeyed God, and consequently material blessing was a sign of God's favour. Unfortunately, this was twisted such that when some Israelites grew rich by oppressing others, they took their wealth as a sign of God's favour. Israel eventually was sent into exile because of her oppression, idolatry, and rejection of God's ways.

But the same laws of blessings for obedience and curses for disobedience do not apply to individual Christians or the Church in the way that they applied to the Israelite nation. Craig Blomberg writes that, 'the wealth of the patriarchs must therefore be understood in its clear covenantal context. The wealth is directly tied to God's plan to give his people a special land.' Abraham's wealth, for example, is 'the first provisional fulfilment of the promise' that God would bless Abraham's descendants. 'The preservation of the patriarchs through Genesis 12-50 is never an end in itself, or primarily a response to their levels of obedience to God, but rather God's sovereign method of fulfilling his promises to gather a unique people together in a unique land.'[152] Nevertheless, we can draw some principles from the wealth of the patriarchs and how they earned and handled their money.

Job

Job was an important man who owned seven thousand sheep, three thousand camels, one thousand oxen and five hundred donkeys. This is a lot by pretty much any standards. In the UK, the average sheep flock size is 420, and the average cow herd size is 90.[153] Only 4 per cent of UK cow farmers have more than 100 cattle. A mixed cattle-and-sheep farmer with 500 animals is very far from Job's 11,500 animals.

Having said that, the UK may not be the best comparator. The UK today is much more densely populated than the Middle East was in Job's day. There simply isn't the space in the UK for livestock farmers to expand their farming by moving onto more land. When Abraham and

Lot had too much livestock for the land on which they were living, they simply moved somewhere else where there were fewer people. This isn't possible in the UK, where land is a valuable commodity because there isn't enough of it for everything that is needed. In other countries, where there is much more land for the population size, flock sizes are much nearer that of Job: in Western Australia, the average sheep herd size is 2,700 and 17 per cent of sheep farms have more than 4,000 sheep. This is still some way from Job's 11,500 animals, but no longer out of reach; it makes him rich, but not obscenely rich.

So Job was a rich and powerful man. He owned a lot of animals and employed a lot of people. But Job's possession of livestock was not a luxury or expensive hobby in the way that rich people today own racehorses. He wasn't buying animals as a status symbol or to enjoy their physical prowess. He wasn't acquiring possessions for his own private enjoyment or simply because he had the money to spend. His animals were the food (meat and milk), clothing (wool and leather), transport, and work-engines of Job's day, crucial to the survival of humanity. In this respect Job was much more akin to our livestock farmers than to our yacht-owners. The animals were part of his business, not his private possessions.

Nor were Job's animals like owning stocks and shares or other assets that bring a high rate of return, often without any active management or productive work. Animals require looking after, which costs money. They can't be left to their own devices, for they will get ill or injured and die, and with that death goes part of the business's wealth and income-generating facility. Job's many animals will have needed many people to look after them, and those people will have come at a price. And Job's business was frighteningly vulnerable to famine, which could wipe out all his livestock and leave him with nothing at all – no income, no wealth, and no means of generating an income.

This may be an important distinction. A successful business is a source of income, but it isn't itself a luxury asset; businesses need to continue, not be consumed. If Job had sold all his animals, he wouldn't merely have converted his possessions into money; he would have destroyed his income source. He could likely have lived off the liquidation of his business for a while, but eventually he would have run out of money, and then what would he have done? He would have thrown away a perfectly good job and left himself vulnerable for no good reason. He'd have to go out and find another job, when there was nothing wrong with his old one. There is no inherent value in leaving a well-paid job for insecurity and poverty.

In contrast, someone who has a large number of assets can sell those assets without affecting his income stream, because selling assets is separate from his normal income derived through paid work. Assets are merely what he did with his income, and they represent a different way of storing money. Selling an asset is a way of releasing money so that it can be used in the economy, whether to buy something else for oneself or to meet the needs or desires of others.

The key question, therefore, is not how much 'wealth' Job had in the form of a successful business, but what he did with this business wealth and his income stream.

Job was widely viewed as blameless and upright, and the greatest man in the land.[154] People respected and listened to him, recognising his views as upright and good.[155] In terms of his business, he always treated his servants fairly and ensured that they got justice.[156] In his personal life, he was pure, not looking lustfully at women or letting his heart wander after another man's wife.[157] And in terms of his own money, he was extraordinarily generous.

Job was respected and commended because of his kindness to those in need. He rescued the poor and defended the stranger; he was eyes to the blind, feet to the lame, and a father to the fatherless.[158] He did not let the poor, widowed, or orphaned grow weary; and nor did he let anyone die for want of clothing, go hungry for want of food, or sleep on the street for want of a home.[159]

Job maintained a conviction in God's faithfulness and our dependence upon him. He never put trust in money and nor did he worship the sun or moon.[160] Whilst Job's children apparently enjoyed multiple feasts a year, even becoming incapacitated through drink, it does not appear that Job participated in such indulgences. Instead, he would arrange for the purification of his children after a period of feasting, and would make burnt offerings on their behalf, that any sin committed whilst feasting might be forgiven (Job 1:5). Far from participating in excessive indulgence of wealth, Job used his income to honour God and deliver his children from divine justice.

When Job lost his children, business, and health, his response was, 'Naked I came from my mother's womb, and naked I will depart. The LORD gave and the LORD has taken away; may the name of the LORD be praised'.[161] The book of Job tells us that, 'In all this, Job did not sin by charging God with wrongdoing'.[162] Job's response shows that he saw his previous prosperity as a gift from God, not a right which he had earned. His position and possessions did not 'belong' to him in any inherent way. Neither his hard work nor his previous good deeds meant that the prosperity he enjoyed was 'his', as opposed to God's. It was God's wealth, and therefore God's right to do anything with it as he chose, including taking it away; and it was Job's responsibility to use it for the good of others.

In Job, therefore, we see someone who is a God-honouring and successful businessman who uses his income, position, and possessions to help others, whether family or stranger, and to deal fairly with all, whether high or low. He does not view the wealth as his own, and does not use it as though it is his own. In both his actions and his attitude, Job shows that the wealth and income he had were not his, but God's. Like Job, any success and prosperity that we enjoy is to be seen as a gift from God to be used for God's glory in the service of others.

Abraham

We first encounter Abraham in Genesis 11, where we are given his genealogy and early history. Abraham left Ur with his father Terah, wife Sarah, and nephew Lot to go to Canaan, but they stopped short of Canaan in Harran and settled there. When Abraham was 75, God called him out of Harran to Canaan, and so Abraham, Sarah, Lot, and all their people and possessions (a term that includes flocks and herds) moved on again. Abraham stopped in Shechem to build an altar to God, and then continued on south through Canaan.

But then there was a famine. This is always a disaster, but especially so for livestock owners. Many of Abraham's animals would have died, taking his business and income source with them. The price of food and even clothing – which was still made from animals and plants – would have gone up, draining any remaining life savings, wealth, and possessions that weren't tied up in living beings. Abraham may have escaped the famine to some extent by going to Egypt, but it is unlikely that he didn't suffer at least some losses.

Going to Egypt resulted in Abraham becoming very wealthy, but not in an honest way. In Egypt, Abraham was afraid that an Egyptian man might desire Sarah, and kill him in order to get her. Rather than lose her through death, Abraham decided to pass her off as his sister (they were half-siblings anyway). Just as Abraham had thought, an Egyptian man did desire Sarah – the Pharaoh. Pharaoh took Sarah into his palace, and gave many animals and servants to Sarah's 'brother' as a sign of his favour. But Sarah was married, and God sent serious disease to Pharaoh's household as a judgment and warning.

Pharaoh clearly paid attention, because he confronted Abraham and sent the two away – with everything that they had.

It is at this point that the Bible tells us that Abraham 'had become very wealthy in livestock and in silver and gold'.[163] At least some of that wealth came from Egypt as a gift from Pharaoh to Sarah's 'brother'. Abraham's wealth therefore came from his lie. That Pharaoh permitted Abraham and Sarah to leave with all of Pharaoh's gifts was an astounding act of grace given Abraham's behaviour. It is a sign of God's blessing on Abraham, but not of approval of Abraham's conduct. Abraham's wealth is not a blessing for obedience but a demonstration of God's extraordinary grace.

Abraham's wealth soon caused problems in his family. Between him and Lot, they simply had too many animals to fit into the land together. The land was over-grazed and over-crowded, and as a result arguments arose between Abraham's herders and Lot's herders. Most likely they were arguing over access to land, grazing, and water. There were only two options available: destroy, sell, or otherwise get rid of some of the animals; or split up. As a consequence of their choice to split up, Lot ended up living near a wicked city, Sodom, from which he had to be rescued twice.

Abraham went to live in Hebron after he and Lot had separated. After Sodom was destroyed, he moved to the area between Kadesh and Shur (still in Canaan) and for a time he stayed in Gerar. Here, he repeated his earlier lie of calling Sarah his sister rather than his wife. The king of Gerar, Abimelech, saw Sarah and took her to be his wife. But God revealed to him in a dream that Sarah was in fact Abraham's wife, and that she must be sent back. In Egypt, Abraham had been given great wealth because he was favoured by Pharaoh as Sarah's brother. In Gerar, Abraham was given great wealth by Abimelech as a covering for the sin against Sarah and to vindicate her in the people's eyes. For a second time, Abraham increased his wealth as a consequence of sin.

Abraham sometimes used his wealth and position wisely. He adjudicated the dispute between his and Lot's herders. He mustered his trained men to rescue Lot when Lot had been taken captive by a conquering group. He refused any gift from the high priest Melchizedek, giving as his reason that no person could say that they had made Abraham rich (although Pharaoh and Abimelech had made Abraham rich). He insisted on asking for God's blessing upon his son Ishmael, even though Ishmael was not the covenant son. When Sarah died, Abraham insisted upon paying a full price for a field in which to bury her, when the owner would have gladly given the field in recognition of Abraham's prestige. And when Abraham was dying, he provided for the sons of his concubines before sending them to live away from Isaac.

But Abraham also failed in his use of wealth. He allowed his wealth to separate him and Lot. He failed to protect Hagar, his wife's servant and mother of his first son, and instead let Sarah drive Hagar away twice. At least some of his wealth was not earned through right conduct or obedience to or trust in God, but was a remarkable act of grace from God after Abraham twice lied about his wife and failed to trust God for protection. Abraham's wealth is not an indicator that it is not problematic for a Christian to be wealthy.

Isaac

Isaac's life is like a copy of his father's. Abraham had been blessed abundantly by God, and when he died he left all that he still possessed to Isaac. Isaac did nothing to deserve all of Abraham's possessions; it was God's gift to Isaac, as God's chosen heir of Abraham.

There was another famine during Isaac's time. God told Isaac not to go down to Egypt – where Abraham had gone during famine, and become wealthy by passing his wife off as just his sister. So Isaac moved only as far as Gerar, where Abraham had for the second time passed Sarah off as his sister, and for the second time become wealthy through it.

Isaac repeated the same deceit. He said to himself, 'The men of this place might kill me on account of Rebekah, because she is beautiful'.[164] So he told people that she was his sister. The Bible tells us that, 'when Isaac had been there a long time, Abimelech [probably the son of Abraham's Abimelech] king of the Philistines looked down from a window and saw Isaac caressing his wife Rebekah. So Abimelech summoned Isaac and said, 'She really is your wife! Why did you say, "She is my sister"?'.[165] He gave orders that no-one was to molest Isaac or his wife Rebekah.

Isaac grew very wealthy in Gerar. So wealthy, that the Philistines in whose land he lived became envious. They filled up all the wells that Abraham had dug, and told Isaac to leave; he had become too powerful for them. Isaac moved a little way and opened up other wells that Abraham had dug, which the Philistines had filled in after Abraham's death. Isaac's herdsmen found more water, but this led to another quarrel with the local herdsmen. Isaac dug another well, but there was quarrelling over that too. So he moved on even further and dug a third well. This time there was no dispute over space and water, so Isaac stayed there, saying 'Now the Lord has given us room and we will flourish in the land'.[166] Here, Abimelech came to him to make a treaty of peace, in recognition that the Philistines had allowed Isaac to leave peaceably among them and grow very wealthy.

Isaac did not benefit as directly as Abraham had from claiming that his wife was his sister, but he gained at least indirectly because it led to Abimelech commanding the Philistines that this foreigner was not to be harmed. Living in a peaceful, stable community makes prosperity much easier to achieve and maintain.

And like Abraham, Isaac discovered that wealth can cause problems with relationships, such that maintaining wealth requires a person to move away from those relationships. Isaac, like Abraham, had control over more livestock than the land had capacity for – he was overgrazing the land and taking more than a fair and reasonable amount of water. He could reduce his usage, or he could move away. He chose to move.

Jacob

Jacob started his adult life by deceiving his father, enraging his brother, and fleeing to the land of his mother.

Jacob was one of twins who, in the womb, had jostled so much that their mother, Rebekah, went to God to ask why. God's answer was that she was pregnant with twins (no ultrasound in those days to reveal two babies!) and that whilst both boys would sire great nations, the younger brother would be stronger than the elder, and be served by the elder. Esau was born first, followed swiftly by Jacob, who was grasping Esau's heel. Isaac loved Esau the most, because Esau was a hunter and Isaac loved to eat wild game. He was led by his stomach. The Bible does not say whether Rebekah told Isaac about the prophecy from God.

Like Isaac, Esau too was led by his stomach. Returning one day from the country, Esau was hungry, and asked Jacob for food. He may have been literally starving. Jacob took advantage of Esau's hunger to use the opportunity to 'sell' the food in return for Esau's birth-right – the double inheritance that belongs to the firstborn son. Jacob should have been confident in God's promise, and not have resorted to manipulation and exploitation of his brother's need. Esau should not have followed his stomach to sell something that was of far greater importance, even if he felt that he was dying and about to lose the inheritance anyway; he too should have trusted in God's provision.

Later, when Isaac was blind and dying, Jacob tricked his father Isaac into giving him the double blessing which Esau should have received as the first-born son. Again, Jacob took his own approach to obtain what God had already promised him, and in so doing both greatly upset his father (who 'trembled violently' when he found out) and his brother, who determined that, once Isaac had died, he would kill Jacob. When their mother learned of this, she told Jacob to flee to her brother, Laban.

It does not appear that Jacob took much with him. Unlike his father, who inherited his wealth from Abraham, Jacob fled his (divinely promised but deceitfully bought) inheritance. He sought refuge with his uncle Laban, who took him into the household and provided for him whilst Jacob worked for Laban. Jacob was paid no wage, but he did get from Laban a promise that he could marry Laban's younger daughter, Rachel. This Jacob did after seven years of living with and working for Laban, albeit after having first been tricked into marrying Rachel's elder sister, Leah. Laban permitted Jacob to marry Rachel a week later, on condition that he would work another seven years for her.

Jacob's family was not happy. His love for Rachel over Leah caused conflict, and God gave children to Leah in her unloved state and not to Rachel. Over several years, Leah bore to Jacob his first four sons: Reuben, Simeon, Levi, and Judah. Rachel, upset, sought to have children by proxy, and gave Jacob her maidservant, Bilhah, as a wife. Bilhah gave birth to Dan and Napthali. Leah in turn became upset and, seeing that she herself had not borne a child for some time (possibly because Jacob had refused to sleep with her), gave her maidservant, Zilpah, to Jacob. Zilpah had Gad and Asher. Leah later had Issachar, Zebulun, and Dinah. Finally, Rachel became pregnant, and gave birth to Joseph.

At this point, Jacob asked Laban for permission to return home. Laban begged Jacob to stay, saying that God had blessed him through Jacob. He offered Jacob wages, and Jacob asked only that he might take all the spotted or speckled sheep and goats. Following some complicated shenanigans and back-stabbing, Jacob ended up with a flock of strong and healthy mottled goats and sheep, whilst Laban's flock was weak and plain. Jacob gained his wealth through deceit and manipulation.

As with his father and grandfather, Jacob found that wealth causes problems with relationships. Laban's sons became upset with Jacob, feeling – to some extent justly – that Jacob had stolen Laban's wealth. Laban also became less friendly towards the man whom he had supported for years and to whom he had given both his daughters. Jacob, for his part, contended that Laban had changed his wages ten times, whilst Rachel and Leah felt that their father no longer cared for them. Jacob fled again, deceiving Laban by not saying that he was going. Laban pursued Jacob, and they argued, finally agreeing that neither would cross onto the other's land to harm the other. Laban also warned Jacob not to mistreat Laban's daughters and grandchildren, as he still had a familial interest in their wellbeing.

Neither Laban nor Jacob behaved honestly. Jacob behaved dishonestly over the matter of the mottled sheep and goats, cheating Laban out of his wealth and prospering at Laban's expense. Laban cheated Jacob over the marriage of Jacob and Rachel, and tried to cheat Jacob in the matter of the sheep and goats. Jacob actually cheated Laban over the sheep and goats, stoked up family discord, and then tried to leave surreptitiously. Although God had promised blessing to Jacob, Jacob was deceitful and dishonourable in the way that he obtained it. It cost him many broken relationships – first with his father and brother, and later with Laban and Laban's other children. Jacob had to leave his mother, and then later take Rachel and Leah away from theirs.

Jacob's wealth did not guarantee him success or security. His favourite son, Joseph, did not get on well with the other sons. Joseph is recorded as bringing a bad report on his brothers to his father, and of boasting of God's promise to him that he would rise above his brothers. The brothers resented Jacob's favouritism and the strongly preferential behaviour towards Joseph. The antagonism became so bad that Joseph's brothers sold him to be a slave in Egypt, and told their father that Joseph was dead. Jacob's prosperity did not bring him a happy family.

Much later, there was a great famine in the land. Jacob's family was so hungry that they had to go to Egypt to beg for food. Jacob's previous wealth was no use in such circumstances. As a livestock owner, famine literally killed his business. Although the famine reunited Jacob with his favourite son, the story of Jacob is one of deceit and family breakdown. It is not a happy story, and it does not show wealth as an acceptable or even desirable situation for a Christian to be in.

David

David started life as the youngest son of a large family. He was the shepherd boy, of little account and overlooked when Samuel came to find a king. In the normal course of life, David would never have been rich or famous.

David's accession to the throne of Israel was through God's favour. Before he got there, he spent many years as an outcast and an exile, in poverty and in danger of losing his life. When he did become king, he spent two years at war with eleven of the twelve tribes of Israel, as at first only Judah recognised his kingship. Much of his kingship was spent in battle with one pagan tribe or another, starting with the Jebusites who at the time lived in Jerusalem.

David's wealth wasn't for himself, but was supposed to be for the good of his people. God commanded that a king should write out for himself the full book of the Law and was to read from it every day.[167] He was particularly commanded to fear God by obeying all the words of the Law. His position should not have made him arrogant or selfish, but was to be used to serve God's people. He should not have accumulated wealth to himself.

David's wealth wasn't because of his merit, and he didn't become wealthy by being a good businessman. He became wealthy by virtue of being made king, and then from the tributes brought to Israel by the pagan tribes and nations that Israel conquered. 2 Samuel 8 lists some of the conquered peoples and the tribute that they gave to Israel and David as Israel's king.

David's wealth was tied up in his kingship. When his son Absalom rebelled against him, David had to flee. His household – all his wives, children, and officials, and most of his concubines – went with him, but at such a time being the head of a large household is more of a hindrance than a help. It is unlikely that they were able to take much with them in the way of clothes, bedding material, and food, when they had to leave swiftly. They are unlikely to have taken any wealth or precious objects with them.

A distant relative of Saul threw stones and dirt at David as his household left Jerusalem, and they arrived at their destination exhausted despite the refreshment given to them by Ziba – who himself had stolen it from Jonathon's crippled son, Mephibosheth, though David did not know that at the time. David had to cross the Jordan, where representatives of the Ammonites and other tribes brought them bedding, bowls, and food, surmising – probably rightly – that David and his followers would be hungry, thirsty, and tired, and lacking in these essential items.

Many of the lessons we derive from David's life relate to his foreshadowing of the true eternal king of Israel, Jesus. Given David's position as the king of what was otherwise a theocracy, it is not always valid to draw direct parallels between his life and ours. As the king of Israel, David was rich, but as an individual he was not. If David's wealth tells us anything, it is that God provides for his kingdom and ultimately will possess and rule over everything, and that one day all peoples and nations will give honour to God.

Solomon

Like David, Solomon was wealthy in his position as king. Again, if Solomon had been deposed, he would have lost access to the wealth of Israel. And also like David, much of Israel's wealth under Solomon was derived from the tributes of other nations.

Although very wise, Solomon was not perfect. After Solomon's death, the people of Israel asked Solomon's son to treat them more kindly than Solomon had when he conscripted men to build the temple and his palace. The implication is that Solomon, to at least some extent, oppressed his people through forced labour. Solomon also had a great many wives and concubines, who eventually led him away from God to the worship of idols.

Solomon's behaviour was not ideal, and his wealth does not mean that God condones the subjection of other nations through tribute or individuals through enforced labour, or that God accepts polygamy. Even his great wisdom did not protect him from the deceitfulness of wealth, which is a danger to us all.

Other wealthy people

Through these six people, we see that wealth in the Bible can be acquired through unacceptable behaviour, and that it frequently leads to conflict. Abraham, Isaac, and Jacob became wealthy through bad behaviour – they deceived others. All three experienced conflict with those around them because of their wealth. David and Solomon were wealthy in their position as kings, not because of individual merit, and both used their position to harm others – David through committing adultery with Bathsheba, and Solomon by conscripting Israelite men to hard labour.

We could also have mentioned Joseph, who was given a position of great power in Egypt and the trappings of wealth that came with it. Like David and Solomon, his wealth at that period was tied up in his position. Like Job, his position and wealth were used to bless and serve others; like Job, he experienced extreme poverty (imprisonment) through no fault of his own – indeed, the imprisonment stemmed from his righteous behaviour in refusing sex with Potiphar's wife. Joseph's later access to wealth was given to him not as a reward or for his own consumption, but specifically for him to use for others. However, he didn't use it well: the famine in the land was used by Joseph as a means to acquire great property to Pharaoh, in contrast with the later Israelite laws of Jubilee and debt release that forbade such accumulation to the wealthy. Several centuries after Joseph, Moses had to give up the wealth he had as an adopted son in Pharaoh's household in order to identify with the Israelite people and lead them out into a desert with the hope of a land of milk and honey (i.e., resources given freely by God through nature as opposed to agriculture).

Daniel was also given a position of power in a pagan

nation, in this case Babylon. Like Joseph, his position was given to him by God that he might use it for good. Like Joseph, he didn't receive riches for righteous behaviour, any more than he suffered for sin: Daniel's suffering in being exiled to a foreign country was due to the general sin around him, not his specific sin; and his suffering in being thrown into a den of lions was precisely because of his righteous, not unrighteous, behaviour. Righteous behaviour can just as well lead to suffering as to riches.

In terms of women, we know that Esther was given a position of great influence which brought with it the enjoyment of luxury. It was a deeply precarious position, as the fate of her predecessor showed, and she was naturally aware of this when she was called upon to use her position to protect her people. But despite the high risk that she could lose everything, including her life, if she stood up for her people, she was willing to use the influence she had to save others. Ruth did not have much to offer, other than the security of returning to her own family when her Israelite husband died; but instead, she chose to support Naomi and follow Naomi's God, enduring poverty as she travelled to Israel and started to glean in Boaz's field. And if we had looked at the New Testament, we could have considered women like Joanna and Lydia, who provided for the needs of Jesus, his disciples, and the early church. These women used their wealth not for themselves, but for God.

USING WEALTH WISELY

Steve Orsillo says, 'The church of Jesus Christ in the western world gave up the right to be called essential or necessary in a society, because it quit living for the sake of giving. It quit giving for the sake of helping. It has to have all these fiscal responsibility things in order to give. 'We can't give to you, we won't have a million dollars in the bank in case there's a rainy day.' Way back in the 1700s, when the Cambridge revival happened the preachers that came out of that revival, they said, 'this is crazy, we just go to church and sit in a building'. And they started prison ministry, they started all of the hospital ministry.'[168] They didn't wait until they had enough money before they helped; they helped straight away.

Steve tells of a man in his church who was helped through the church's drug recovery ministry and Steve's leadership – even fathership – of those in his church. Steve says, 'B went through a lifetime of cooking dope and in and out of prison. Now I have known him about 17 years. B hasn't used dope once in 17 years... What would [B] do if I had to have a retirement? What would he do if I wouldn't pay the price... use my spare time?... It's still about doing, and when it's done I don't regret a thing.'[169] Steve does not consider his income and time to belong to himself, but to people like B, who would not make it if Steve were not willing to serve and use what he has to help others.

Another member of Steve's church gave up a sports career in order to serve one of the men taking part in the church's drug rehabilitation programme. The church member had been offered a sponsorship to move to a different part of the USA to play sport, but he knew how much this individual was gaining from his support. What would happen to him if he left? He knew the answer: the person concerned would return to drugs, and would die. Realising his responsibility for his brother, a responsibility given by God, he gave up his career and stayed in Oroville. The young man survived and graduated from rehab – but even if he had fallen back, it would still have been the right thing to do for the church member to stay.

Steve says he sometimes sees people who have served the poor, but got taken advantage of so they quit and have not served again. 'Well,' says Steve, 'you were probably there for the wrong reason. You were there to feed yourself; a pat on the back; a good feeling... [Instead] be there for the reason of helping them. I was there to feed the hungry, and the hungry got fed... I'm not there for them to be nice to me. I'm there to feed them, and they got fed.'[170] When rich people talk of the dignity of helping others as an argument for why charity is better than state support, they promote their own feelings over the feelings of the recipients.'[171] This is not right, as Rabbi ben Maimon also recognised.

God's concern for the wellbeing of the financially poor over the wellbeing of – and even justice for – the better-off is seen in God's challenge to Steve Orsillo when thousands of dollars' worth of property was stolen from his construction company.[172] Steve tells of how he ordered some front doors, at $1200 each, for some properties he was building. A staff member arranged to have the doors delivered at the car shop next to the church, rather than at Steve's house where Steve normally arranged for items to be delivered. This was in a deeply poor and deprived area. Steve knew, as soon as the staff member told him where the doors had been delivered, that the doors would have been stolen by the time Steve got there. Steve also knew who was likely to have stolen the doors. He started to drive round the neighbourhood, seeing whose doors most needed replacing, in order to find where his doors would end up. Then, he says, 'the Lord spoke to me and said, "What are you doing?" I said, "I'm looking for my doors". He said, "whose doors?". I stopped, because the

Lord was speaking, and I'm very reverent to him, and said to him, "But Lord, if they're your doors, why did you want them stolen?" "Whose doors are they? Yours or mine?" and I said, "They're your doors, and you can give them to anyone you want".

Steve turned his truck round, went back to the job site and ordered some more doors. God's concern for the poor trumped his concern for the profit of Steve's company and even for our strict, narrow ideas of justice.

Money

I don't think we can ever over-estimate the deceitfulness of wealth. David is described as a man after God's own heart, but wealth led him into selfishness, idleness, adultery, and conspiracy to kill. Solomon was the wisest person to have ever lived, but was led astray by his wealth and wives. Abraham and Jacob acquired wealth through deceit, and for them as well as Isaac their wealth led to problems with their relatives or neighbours. The Israelites as a nation turned away from God every time they prospered.

The purpose of wealth is to use it for others. Otherwise it corrupts.

I heard a speaker say once that, 'the Bible never says that there's anything wrong with living your life or having money. Those things in and of themselves aren't wrong. There's a difference between working hard and trying to make life work as well as you can, and being so obsessed with those things that you don't leave room for Jesus and his word... It's not wrong to have a nice house and decorate it well, but if we become so obsessed with those things that our eyes and our hearts are taken off Jesus and his words then it becomes a problem.'[173]

I think he was wrong. Speaking to a middle-class

church, with middle-class definitions or expectations regarding 'nice' and 'decorated well', the speaker's words tell them it's okay to live like the rest of the world and not to stand out; to aspire to the same level of comfort as the surrounding middle-class. It says that we aren't called to be a light shining in the darkness, a beacon of generosity, showing the world the way of the cross – of sacrifice – and that instead we can expect to enjoy the fruits of the prosperity gospel. Speaking to a working-class or immigrant church, these words encourage us to aspire to middle-class-ness. They say that we can aim for material things, like the rest of the world. That the way of God is to be middle-class. That the gospel is the prosperity gospel and prosperity means more than what I have now.

The key question for every aspect of our lives – for how we make money, how we treat others, and what we do with the time, energy, and money that we have – is 'how can I honour God with this?' It is the opposite of how we naturally think, which is to neglect to consider the full impact of our actions on others or the extent to which they honour God. We too easily focus on our own needs when God's radical command is that we focus on the needs of others. We too easily think that we have to work to supply our needs, when God says that we are to look to him – and therefore don't need to store up large amounts of wealth for our future selves. So when we lie on our beds, we should not be planning our next purchase. We should be worshipping God. We should be asking God how we can use our wealth to bless others. We should be considering how we can best serve.

If we own a car, how are we using it to glorify God? We could sell it and use the proceeds to help the poor. Or we could use the car to give lifts to people who need help getting around, or lend it to someone whose own car has just broken down or who can't afford one regularly. If we own a house, we could downsize and use the released money or savings from a lower mortgage to do something that helps the people around us. Or we could use any spare rooms to take in someone who needs a home: a care leaver; a failed asylum seeker; a young homeless person; a child in care; a person with low income. If we have children, we could send them to a private school or buy a house near to a good state school – or we could send them to the local school and get involved with the running of that school and provision of homework and afterschool clubs. That way we can ensure not only that our children get a good academic education, but so do poor children, and our children also learn to see the poor as 'us' rather than 'them'.

If we have money, what do we do with it? John Wesley, living in the eighteenth century, set himself a maximum limit on his personal expenditure which he never exceeded, even as his income grew.[174] He determined that a single man could live on £28/year, and stuck to that even when his income reached £1,400/year. It is reported that he never had more than £100 at any one time. For today, an equivalent income for a single person could be around £16,000 after housing costs, in order to allow people to participate adequately in society.[175] To get by on just the barest essentials – which would mean things like keeping the house colder than one would like; buying cheaper and less-nice food; relying on charity clothes rather than new; restricting one's travel; spending less on personal goods – costs at least £120/week after housing.[176] In contrast, people who spend 35 hours each week looking for work receive less than £91/week from a government that has not bothered to ensure that there are enough jobs for all the people who want and are capable of work – and some of that has to go on topping-up inadequate support for rent and council tax.

I am not averse to having some savings: God may have a specific issue or person in mind that he wishes me to give that money to, or it may be that he is aware that I will need it shortly. This is like the ant – or indeed the Israelites – storing up food for winter: when food is seasonal, some has to be set aside to get you through the rest of the year. Modern UK incomes tend not to be seasonal in that way, but there are seasonal changes in expenditure (such as higher heating costs in winter; the cost of school uniforms, shoes, and coats at the start of a new school year; the cost of family gatherings at Christmas) and also some expenditures that are larger but less frequent, such as roof repairs, which might need saving for. At the same time, we shouldn't all need to save for huge costs, because, as Christians, we should help one another out. If this year Alice is helped to have her roof replaced, perhaps next year it will be Brian who is helped to adapt his house for elderly or disabled relatives to move in. By sharing our surplus, we can all have enough without anyone going in need whilst others store up large amounts.

In my own life, at those times when I've had a high enough income to have savings, I have aimed for around 1-2 months' expenditure in my bank account at any one time (£1100-2200). This is enough to cover the highest costs that I am likely to incur, such as replacing my boiler or one of my mobility scooters. Money above that level can be given away, or at least mentally allocated for giving in case God has a future rather than immediate purpose for it. Being in the habit of setting aside some money each month means that I both have money available to donate above my committed giving when God asks for it, and that I can save up quickly when an urgent cost occurs for myself, or replace savings spent on such a cost. The same principle can be applied for people with both higher incomes and higher costs; I don't have children, for example, and my housing situation means I'm not responsible for replacing my roof. Other people may need to set money aside for things like replacing a roof, but it is still worth establishing an upper limit for one's savings congruent with the largest costs that are likely to occur; and to also be willing to give away that saved money when asked to do so by God.

In practice, my income does not always permit me to have savings. To the extent that I do, it is largely because of the generosity of my family in paying for travel and leisure costs, and bailing me out when unaffordable expenses do occur. I am incredibly grateful to my family for supporting me in a lifestyle above what is achievable on benefits alone, and for the security that their generosity gives me. At the same time, the nature of being reliant on charity in that way means that I am acutely aware of every spending decision that I make and the risk that I need help from my family in the future if I spend too much now. This is another reason why justice beats charity. An adequate income provided as of right does not put the same emotional constraints on a person as to whether it is okay to buy treats, or heat the house to a comfortable degree, or have a pet or an enjoyable hobby.

I do not think we can over-estimate the faith-raising potential of great generosity – the level of generosity Jesus calls us all to. Many of the great Christians whose biographies are so inspiring lived radically generous lives. What does this tell us about what Christians should aim for? This is why it saddens me every time I hear a sermon on wealth which tries to excuse the level of consumption enjoyed by middle class Christians. It sounds to me like the deceitfulness of wealth at work. It sounds to me like a weak faith at risk of being strangled, and letting others be strangled too.

I wonder also how it sounds to a poor Christian. Are we telling them that God's desire for their life is that they obtain a middle-class income and living standard? Such a prosperity gospel should be condemned. Are we telling them that Christians are meant to be selfish people on whose lives there is no call to help those in need? This is blasphemy against God's character.

Wealth is deceitful. It needs to be strangled before birth.

Community

A big part of what we do with our money and resources, and who we are as people, is how we live in community. Community is important: we are social beings, who need social interaction; and we are also dependent beings, with all of us relying on the work and goodwill of others in order to get by. This is particularly true for poorer people, who cannot buy-in the replacements for community that richer people can. When middle-class people move out into the suburbs, they forsake the poor and their own role in community. When middle-class people claim that government welfare has undermined community, what they mean is that their own wealth and their ability to live in richer areas has left them ignorant of the ongoing need for community for everyone, and in particular the poor.

When people are in need, that is often the hardest time to be trying to source support. When you are sick and need someone to buy you some food; when you are exhausted with young children and need someone to cook you a meal; when you have run out of money and are ashamed or scared to go to the foodbank; when your marriage has broken down and you're torn up inside; when you've just lost your job and are bewildered and frightened; when the boiler has broken or the pipes have burst and your home is uninhabitable – these are not the times for calmly getting onto the internet and searching for advice. These are the times when you need established friends who can clean your bathroom, buy your shopping, take you in, and hold you together. These are the times when you need to already know the place to turn and not be embarrassed to go there. These are the times when you need community.

Christians should seek to be and build that community. It doesn't matter how much government provision of public services there is; how equal the country; how strong and supportive the welfare state. There is always a need for love, mercy, generosity, and relationship. We are social beings, and whilst the government can ensure that the foundation and basic structure is there, it cannot be the relationships that we need. It can ensure that there are enough houses, doctors, teachers, and criminal barristers; but it can't be your friend who helps you apply for social housing, receive a cancer diagnosis, understand your homework, or support you through a trial (whether as victim or perpetrator). If you can't access affordable housing, die whilst waiting for healthcare, don't get extra support at school, or have to wait years and spend all your money to receive justice, then the burden on your local community is much bigger. But the need for community doesn't go away just because the government is meeting its responsibility. No matter how good it is at its own job, the government is no substitute for friends, family, and community.

Much of what a community does for one another

is intensely practical and cannot be done over a phone or internet connection. Someone the other side of the country may be able to share my emotional burdens, but they can't cook my tea, walk my dog, give me a lift to a medical appointment, or come with me to a social security assessment. Christians therefore need to think carefully about the impact that where they live has on how they can serve God. Some Christians find that this means going abroad to much poorer countries. The rest may find merely that they move to a poorer part of their own country, maybe even of the same local authority. The current pattern – of Christians congregating in middle-class and richer areas – is not a Godly pattern and is surely not what we would see if all Christians sincerely asked God where he wanted them to live and serve.

Moving to a new area is a great opportunity to get to know neighbours. It is an excuse to knock on people's doors to introduce yourself, and to invite them over for tea or coffee or, if it's more your style or theirs, go to the local pub for a drink. Christmas is another good opportunity, if you invite people to your home for Christmas drinks and food, or take a card and a small gift to each of your neighbours. If you have Muslim neighbours, you could bake them some ma'amool to mark the end of Ramadan. Or in summer, you might host a barbecue, or hand out flowers or vegetables grown in your back yard. If you have children, then you're likely to be able to get to know the children and parents in your local area as you see them regularly at the school gate and your children start to make friends. I don't have children, but I know many of the children on my street because I had them over at Christmas for a party the first year I moved in, and then seemed to have them over many afternoons until Covid struck and they were no longer allowed to come into my home and play games. But that initial party started relationships that are still going now.

Once you are friends with your neighbours, it's easy to start to serve. Some of my neighbours struggle to maintain their gardens, so I and people from my local church help to clear the brambles and nettles and rank grass. Sometimes I can't walk my dog, so a neighbour takes him out for me. Another neighbour will invite me over for a meal, or send the children over with a plate of cooked food. One of my closest neighbours takes all sorts of odds and ends off my hands, and is also a good source for things I might need or want – like when I was offered a wheelie-bin full of soft, loose soil for my garden!

As you get to know an area and your neighbours, other things come to light that take a community to address. There might be a problem with litter, or with hedges left to straggle onto pavements or footpaths. There might be difficulties locally with gangs or a lack of things for young people to do. The local school might be struggling, and parents may find it difficult to juggle work with childcare. Christians should be willing to get stuck in with these problems. This doesn't mean every Christian is involved with every issue, but if you look for them, opportunities to serve should come up. If you're a parent, then maybe it is working with your local school or helping with homework or after-school clubs. If you're a gardener, maybe it's helping with your neighbours' gardens. If you have a dog, maybe you help look after a neighbour's dog as well from time to time, or pick up litter and abandoned dog poo on your daily walks. Maybe this will build into community litter-picks, or a group of people helping to overhaul a garden or redecorate a house.

An alternative approach is to get involved in a charity that supports poor people. This may be particularly appropriate if you otherwise live in a richer area, and don't have much contact with people on low incomes. There are many charities around and it is not hard to pick one to volunteer with. You may find that you only need to commit one evening a month; or it might be that by reducing your hours of work by half a day you not only have time to volunteer weekly for a couple of hours but also have more time for your family – and are more refreshed when you do work. Getting involved with a charity over the longer term is a great way to start to get to know the structural issues behind poverty. Then after a while you might find that you naturally want to share what you know with others and talk to local councillors, MPs, and government ministers about the issues to help reduce those contributing factors that are under society's (government's) control.

It takes time to join or help to form a community. If you find that you lack time, then maybe you could reconsider your work commitments. Perhaps you should reduce your hours of work. This might necessitate moving to a cheaper house – but perhaps you have already done that, as you moved to a poorer area to live and serve there. Perhaps you are very busy with church commitments – and maybe you need to think about the balance between religiosity (what the Pharisees did right) and practical service (which the Pharisees forgot). You may also need to consider whether your children need to live a middle-class lifestyle with multiple social engagements. On my street, hobbies aren't a major feature, and when they are present, it is usually a single after-school event rather than evening or weekend event. This means that evenings and weekends are still free for friends, family, and neighbours. The children play on the street, call round for their friends, and even pop into my house for a boardgame or some baking. In contrast, I find that for my middle-class friends – and I remember from my own upbringing – evenings rapidly fill up once church and hobbies have been catered for. There is little time left for the actual practical side of loving other people.

It takes time and commitment to be a part of community. It cost Jesus the glories of heaven and 33 years of confinement to a limited body – quite a major step for an omnipresent, omnipotent, omniscient God. But God couldn't have community with us by any other way. We can't expect community to be easy, quick, or non-sacrificial either.

Poverty

When those of us with wealth consider what we are to do with it, a natural question to ask is who are the poor and why are they poor. In some instances, this is used as an excuse to refuse to help. More appropriately, it is used to understand what is the form of help that is needed. When we understand why poverty exists and why particular people are poor, then we better understand what to do about it. This is particularly important when we are looking for long-term answers that prevent poverty, and not just short-term crisis responses that alleviate poverty when we see it. Understanding poverty therefore helps us to understand how we are to live as Christians with the resources that God has given us.

Work ethic

One of the biggest lies of inequality is that poverty is the fault of the poor for not working hard enough, for spending frivolously, or for living unwisely. If this were true, poverty would have been ended long ago, for the poor work very hard. But it is not true. The view that says that poverty is due to 'differences in fundamentals, such as ability, talent or motivation'[177] is unsupported. Instead, a large-scale study set in Bangladesh found that there is 'a threshold level of initial assets above which households accumulate assets, take on better occupations and grow out of poverty' whilst 'the reverse happens for those below the threshold.'[178] Poverty perpetuates poverty.

People living in poverty are sincere in wanting a better life.[179] This includes work and good family relationships. It does not necessarily mean moving away to a 'better' area, but instead the hope of enjoying a better life where one already is. It does not necessarily mean aspiring to go to university, but hoping that the 'job for life' industry and trades that have been decimated by governments since the 1980s would be restored to the UK and allow working class people to take pride in their work again.

People whose only experience of work is of low-wage, high-pressure work in bad conditions nevertheless prefer work to living on benefits or being dependent on family. Young adults who have seen their parents struggle with insecure employment are keen to avoid the same fate themselves, just as their parents want them to do better. People living with chronic illness who are unable to work still want to work, if only they were able. Sick people are forced to work beyond the limits of their health in order to support themselves, and poor people are forced into jobs that make them sick. Yet the work ethic remains strong; it is tenacious in the face of both bad jobs and ill-health.

Poverty in the UK is not primarily, or even largely, because people in poverty have the wrong attitudes and became poor as a consequence. It is because businesses don't pay enough nor provide decent conditions of work; because the government does not ensure full employment and therefore people are left without work, without enough work, or having to spend large portions of their earnings on excessive travel to work and childcare; and because when people do have to depend on social security, the government does not provide anything like an adequate income. It is because it is not possible to move house to find work if you are dependent on social housing for affordability, because a new housing area won't accept you without several years' living or working in that area – which you can't get until you live there. It's because it is not possible to move house to find work if you are dependent on family for childcare, or your family needs you to care for them in their illness or disability. It's because you can't recover from illness if you are forced to keep working whilst ill just to maintain an inadequate income, because the alternative is destitution on the UK benefits system.

Understanding money

Repeated studies confirm that poor people know how to handle money (it is not poor spending choices that make them poor) and even understand the value of money better than do rich people.[180] Consider this thought experiment. You are lying on a hot beach with only water to drink, and you'd love a beer. Your friend gets up to go and buy a beer, and offers to get one for you too from the only place nearby which sells beer. But neither of you knows what the beer will cost, so you give your friend a maximum that you're willing to spend. How much would you be willing to spend if the shop was a small run-down corner shop, and how much would you be willing to spend if it came from a smart resort?[181]

Consider another thought experiment. You bought a multi-game ticket for your favourite sports team. The ticket costs £160 and specifies eight games that you can attend on that ticket, which individually usually cost £30. Now the season is nearly over and you have one game left on your ticket. There is a lot of excitement about this game, and tickets are selling for £75. You are about to go to the game. How do you feel about the cost of the game?

In the first thought experiment, richer people were more likely to suggest a higher maximum price for a beer from a trendy resort than a beer from a run-down shop, even though the two beers are the same. Poorer people have a better concept of the value of the beer, and are better at setting aside irrelevant contextual factors. In the second experiment, richer people were more likely to say that the game cost them £20, the price at which they originally bought the ticket. Many will even say that it costs £0, because they've already paid. The real cost is £75, because this is the money that is foregone because of the decision to attend the game rather than sell the ticket. Poor people are much more likely to say that it feels as though attending the game cost them £75. They understand the value of money. Even when economists are asked the question, the easy majority get the answer wrong. And they're meant to understand about opportunity costs!

The very poorest in the UK are often adept at juggling money, surviving off charity shops, food clubs, and money-off deals, but that does not get them out of poverty. Instead, it leaves them emotionally, cognitively, and often physically exhausted, and strips them of capacity to engage in activity that might boost their work opportunities, let alone invest in their children's education. The mental load associated with poverty can lower a person's IQ by 10-

13 points, enough to take someone from normal to sub-normal; and it drains the executive control and decision-making power that is needed to make choices or manage a household.[182]

Decision making

People in poverty may be more likely to be experiencing the kinds of things that can influence us towards decisions that have short-term gain but long-term problems. When we are cold, tired, hungry, or stressed then our bodies and brains may favour decisions that bring short-term relief rather than deciding to continue to experience suffering in the hope that this leads to a better future. Indeed, such delayed gratification may be a costly rather than beneficial behaviour, with immediate gratification more likely to be the adaptively superior behaviour. We are not robots, and the permanent denial of pleasure is not viable for us.

The problem for poor people is that we don't have the financial flexibility to afford to let our physical and emotional state have input into our purchases, but these states operate at subconscious levels, and repeatedly over-riding them is exhausting. Rich people can get away with giving into short-term needs, but poor people can't. Rich people may then think that it is their superior restraint that keeps them rich, rather than realising that it is their riches that allow them to get away with lapses in restraint.

I was asked recently for my thoughts on giving money to someone who then spends it frivolously. My answer was that if you think that the money has been spent frivolously, then you haven't given enough. You haven't given enough money to make a meaningful difference to that person's life in the long-term. You haven't given enough money to cover the deposit on the rent of a nicer house with a better landlord. You haven't given enough money for buying a new boiler. You haven't given enough money for the cost of further education. All you've given is enough money to make that person's life a little bit more bearable in the here and now.

It is hard being poor. You can spend many days being cold, exhausted, hungry, stressed, and worn down. It may have been weeks since there was a warm day with a blue sky. You may not be able to afford to have friends over for a cup of tea. You may not enjoy the food you eat, because you eat mostly what you are given by charity or is on offer at the shops. There may be extremely little in your life that gives you joy, and you may find yourself craving something – anything – to bring some pleasure. It is even worse if you have children and you know that their life is also bleak and cold. In these circumstances, when someone gives you a small amount of money, it is adaptively sensible to spend that money on something that brings you or your family pleasure. It is appropriate to take action that helps to keep you sane, boost your mood, and reduce some of the harmful impacts of constant poverty.

For poor people, there is little or nothing to be gained from setting money aside for a hypothetical future which your and your peers' experience tells you will never come. For richer people to tell poor people to live like this is highly cruel. We cannot require poor people to live as though they are middle-class, making decisions that are adaptive for the middle-class environment, whilst leaving them in the very environments for which these behaviours are not suited.

CONCLUSION

It is easy when one has money to deceive oneself as to one's right to keep that money. We seek to praise ourselves for our hard work and castigate others for being lazy. But the evidence is against the idea that poverty is caused by people being lazy, having unhealthy lifestyles, or making bad spending decisions. Instead, poverty is caused by insufficient jobs so that some people are left unemployed; by bad jobs that make people ill; and by insufficient money to cover any spending mistakes or to make saving for a better future an adaptively superior response.

Christians need to actively fight against the deceitfulness of wealth. Of course, it is much more pleasant for us if we can lay an outright claim to our salary, and can ignore poor people on the basis that their poverty is self-induced. But neither the Bible nor the evidence on the causes of poverty make such selfishness excusable before God.

CHAPTER 6

THE SIN OF
THE PEOPLE

IMAGINE HOW YOU WOULD feel if you were a Hebrew slave under the Egyptians, and heard Moses try to evade God's command that he free the slaves. 'Who am I, Lord?' asks Moses, 'and who are you? Who will listen to me, and what will they think of me? What skills and qualifications do I have for this role?'[183] Ash Barker, who suggested this line of thinking, comments that, 'Moses wanted to raise his young family, keep working, and live as normal a life as possible.'[184] His own comfort was a higher priority to him than the suffering of many people.

How do you think the world would feel if it understood the nature of Christianity, yet saw Christians refuse to live that way? How do the poor and oppressed feel when the Church does little to relieve poverty and says nothing about injustice? The presentation that poor people are given is of a God who does not care about their suffering and is not interested in justice. Yet that is not the God we follow.

Amongst the Western evangelical church, possibly the most common mistake is Pharisaism: knowing the doctrine and doing the ritual and even the private holiness of relationship with God, but missing the practical righteousness – and being completely unaware of this failure. The Pharisees carried out the letter of the law on cleanliness and sacrifice, but neglected social justice. Much to their surprise, Jesus condemned them for it.

The Pharisees' error was not novel. The Israelites had tried it many times before. My childhood understanding of the sin of the Israelites was that they repeatedly stopped worshipping God in order to worship false gods and live as they pleased, and repeatedly had to be brought back to God through the prophets and the discipline of being conquered by foreign nations. The easy application was: don't stop worshipping God. Don't be a pagan or an atheist. As an extra assurance, don't be sexually impure.

But to read the history of the Israelites like that is to misunderstand their and our situation. The sins of which God accused the Israelites were not that they had become pagans and that they no longer had anything to do with him at all. Rather, their sin was in attempting to serve foreign powers, worship false gods, and live selfish and oppressive lives at the same time as offering the ritualistic elements of worship to the one true God. The message of the Old Testament is not that we shouldn't be like the pagan, unbelieving Israelites. It is that we shouldn't be like the God-fearing, God-believing, God-seeking Israelites who still misunderstood who God is and what he wants from his people.

Adrian Plass tells a parable in which a young man seeking to join a new version of Christianity complains that its sole requirement – to climb Snowdon three times a week – is too hard.[185] The man with whom he is speaking replies that he misunderstands. This new approach is much, much easier than real Christianity. It is much easier to make weekly sacrifices to a deity than it is to live with Jesus in every part of your life. It is much easier to be in an idolatrous relationship in which humanity gives to a deity in order to receive something back, than it is to be in a right relationship with the one true God. It is much easier to give a sum of money to a charity than it is to invite a poor person to live in your home.

Jesus was right to warn us to 'be on your guard against the yeast of the Pharisees, which is hypocrisy'.[186] Like them, it is easy to think that we are right in our doctrine and application, yet be ignorant of the extent to which the lack of economic justice, practical righteousness, or public holiness in our lives is a matter so serious that it can call into question our salvation. Jesus called the Pharisees hypocrites, vipers, and white-washed tombs. If we are to avoid the same judgment on us, it is vital that we have a full understanding of how God calls us to live.

REJECTING GOD

The biggest theme in the message of the prophets is that God's people have rejected him. This is spoken of in general language, leaving us to study the rest of the prophets' writings to understand what precisely it means to reject God. This is particularly important, because the Israelites tended to continue to worship God in terms of all the religious rites and rituals. Yet God still claimed that they had rejected him. If religious observances – church attendance, and Bible study, and prayer, and praise – are not enough to say that one follows God, then it is vitally important that we ask God what it does mean to follow him.

God made us to live in relationship with and worship him. When we reject him as the one who is in authority over us, we reject the natural order of things. 'The ox knows its owner, and the donkey its master's manger', but Israel did not know her master.[187] 'Even the stork in the sky knows her appointed seasons, and the dove, the swift and the thrush observe the time of their migration.' But God's people all too often do not know the requirements of the Lord.[188]

Again and again in the prophets, it was declared of Israel that no-one listened, she said she would not listen, they did not listen, they refused to listen. The Israelites did not want to listen to the prophets that God sent them. They told God's prophets to be quiet, or to prophesy only positive things.[189] They thought that they were wise, on the grounds that they had the word of God, but despite that they did not really know the requirements of God.[190]

The Israelites knew that God defends those who honour him, and they thought that they did indeed honour him and that therefore his words would do good to them. They knew of God's commands regarding religious behaviours, but missed that God demands more than this.[191] They were unaware of their sin, or that God considers the accumulation and seeking-after of wealth to be evil and wicked theft.

Even after their exile and subsequent return to Judah, God's people did not love him fully. They brought blemished animals for sacrifice, and so defiled the Lord's table.[192] They failed to bring all of the tithe owed to God, thinking that they could get away with a tokenistic fraction of what was due.[193] Instead of joyfully giving back to God out of recognition of his provision and glory, they complained that the sacrifices were burdensome, and offered the least they thought they could get away with.[194] The men married women who worshipped false gods,[195] and divorced their

(Jewish) wives.[196] They ignored God's laws of justice and twisted God's words to make them sound as though they permitted evil and injustice.[197] They did all of this yet were unaware of their sin[198] and wondered why God did not bless them.[199]

They thought that they were righteous, when in fact they had wearied God.[200] They complained that it was futile to serve God fully,[201] when they were guilty of idolatry, sexual immorality, and oppression of the poor and the unprotected.[202] They were ignorant of their sin even as they thought they were obedient, and so they decided that seeking God was futile.

Although they professed repentance and may have truly believed it, they did not apply what they already knew of God's word to their lives. They should have known that they were not to worship false gods, marry outside of their faith, or break faith with their spouse.[203] They should have known not to lie, defraud the worker, oppress the undefended, block the foreigner from accessing justice, or show partiality in judgment.[204] Yet they did all these things, and did not repent of them. The law of God was before them, open for them to read and obey, and all their sacrifices and protestations of humility and repentance meant nothing whilst they did not actually apply God's law to their lives.

God is constantly reaching out to us, offering forgiveness to those who repent and showing mercy in giving us time to do so. But whether they were shown grace or discipline, the Israelites kept failing to repent and return to God. 'When grace is shown to the wicked, they do not learn righteousness; even in a land of uprightness they go on doing evil and do not regard the majesty of the Lord'.[205] When Israel was shown blessing and given all she needed, she did not praise or thank God for it.[206]

When she was disciplined and suffered drought, famine, or attack, she did not turn to God for help.[207] And after she had been graciously returned to her land following exile, she still declared that it was futile to follow God, because when she (half-heartedly) sought him he did not listen.[208]

When we seek to follow God, we must do so with our whole selves and everything that we have. Our emotions, understanding, and strength should all be devoted to him. All of our time, energy, and possessions should be considered as belonging to him. We must study his ways so that we can know what he wants and live in accordance with it. Without that, we do not truly acknowledge God as our Lord and Master, and we cannot truly worship him.

RELIGIOUS RITES

God's prophets were often called to condemn the behaviour of God's people even as God's people thought that they were doing right. They still brought sacrifices and burnt offerings to God; they continued to hold the New Moon festivals, Sabbath days and feasts; and they still prayed to God, held fasts, and assembled together to worship him.[209] They thought that their feasts, assemblies, songs of worship, sacrifices, and offerings meant that they were in a right relationship with God and were obedient to his will.[210] They thought that as long as they had the temple of the Lord, they were safe.[211] But they were not.

The indictment is not that the Israelites did not follow the sacrificial laws at all, but that they did so without bringing the rest of their lives into alignment with God. The Israelites still said the right things, honouring God with their words, but because of their failure in other areas, their religion was only words and not of the heart.[212] They took oaths in God's name, but did not do so in truth and righteousness;[213] he was 'near to their lips but far from their mind'.[214] He was so far from their minds, that the richer members took their prosperity as a sign of blessing from God and confirmation that they were not guilty of sin.[215] They thought that they were righteous and obedient, when God was so wearied of their sin that he was preparing for their exile. They were sufficiently unaware of their wrongdoing that they queried why God was bringing disaster upon them.[216]

Though they continued in the sacrifices and rituals of God's law, this did not make the Israelites clean and holy as they believed.[217] They committed murder, theft, adultery, perjury, and idolatry, yet thought that they could come before God and say, 'We are safe', because they had the Temple and sacrificial system.[218] They disobeyed the word of God, yet thought that their possession of the word of God made them wise.[219]

Religious rituals were never all that God wanted. God wanted the Israelites to behave justly and righteously.[220] As long as they oppressed the vulnerable, exploited the poor, and followed false gods they were not acceptable before God, however much worship they brought.[221] By living unjust, oppressive, and idolatrous lives, they had made God's house into a den of robbers.[222] By failing to enact justice and shalom, the Israelites divided themselves from God and became wicked and iniquitous people with blood on their hands.[223] Humility, sacrifice, and praise are worse than nothing to God when they are not accompanied by actions to defend the poor and achieve economic justice. They are instead a stench which God cannot stand;[224] no better than the abomination of killing a person as a sacrifice or the defilement of offering a pig.[225]

God said that Israel was circumcised in the flesh

but not in the heart, and that therefore the circumcision of the flesh was meaningless. The true circumcision that God wants is obedience to him through justice and the rejection of false gods, not the outward rituals whilst continuing to be unjust and pursuing wealth and power. Whilst circumcision is open to both Jews and Gentiles, it is also the case that the outward rite alone will not save either Jew or Gentile.[226] Sacrifices for sin don't wash away our guilt if we don't turn away from that sin.[227]

In the end, even the rituals that God prescribed are not what he wants.[228] God wants 'mercy, not sacrifice, and acknowledgement of God rather than burnt offerings'.[229] He wants his people to sow righteousness by returning to God, maintaining love and justice, and waiting for God.[230] If we did this, then we would reap unfailing love.[231] God's people must turn away from dependence upon secular powers, reject home-made gods, and seek forgiveness.[232]

Compared to what God wants – that we know him, trust him, and believe in him by obeying him – the sacrifices he asked for are iniquitous and deeply unclean.[233] God needs nothing from us and we can give him nothing, for everything – even the animals for the sacrifice and the stones of the altar – were made by him and belong to him already. The offerings that the Israelites made to God were like a thief seeking to sell to you something they had just stolen off you. We can only offer ourselves and our worship – our loyalty shown in the obedience and honour we give to God.

FALSE GODS

After general rejection of God, the next most common themes in the prophets about Israel's sin are her allegiance to false gods (over 100 verses in Isaiah, Jeremiah and Ezekiel alone), and her economic injustice and oppression.

Verses on Israel's allegiance to false gods include references to the sacrifices they offered, physical idols they made, and adultery that they thereby committed against God. In many places this allegiance to fake gods is described not only as adultery but as prostitution and harlotry. The comparison to sexual sin is meant to make us as horrified about idolatry as God expects us to naturally be about human adultery.

Although they continued to follow the religious rites of God, the Israelites added in obedience to and worship of false gods. They took on the rites and superstitions of the pagan nations around them.[234] This included worshipping gods that they themselves had created, even making idols out of the same wood which they used for fire, and the same gold that they used for buying and selling.[235] They worshipped the created thing when they should have only worshipped the creator,[236] and put their trust in false gods rather than the true God.[237] The Israelites also went to spiritualists and mediums, when they should have looked to God and his word.[238]

The Israelites made a mockery of the Judaic sacrificial system by offering sacrifices to false gods. Where sacrifices to God are made in recognition of our sin, the ultimate need for justice, and our inability to make ourselves right before God, sacrifices to false gods are about appeasing and pleasing a capricious deity in the hope of blessing. The former is divine grace from an infinitely loving and just God who wants to restore relationship with us; the latter is an attempt to purchase relationship. The former is the only way that we can have access to God, looking forward as it does to Jesus' death in our place; the latter is man's way of getting to the deities by bribes.

The Israelites treated God the same way that they

treated the fake gods. They thought that all that was needed for the appeasement of God was that they offer sacrifices and call on his name.[239] If all that was needed was a sacrifice, then the Israelites could otherwise live as they pleased. But the sacrifice was not about buying God's forgiveness or blessing, but rather was meant to be part of sincere repentance that looked forward to the day when Jesus would take our punishment in our place. So when they said to God 'My Father, my friend from my youth, will you always be angry?'[240] the Israelites failed to recognise that his anger was not that they hadn't brought him enough gifts or appeased his pride by showing him more honour than they showed to other gods, but that they didn't bring their whole lives into line with God.

We cannot follow God at the same time as following false gods.[241] We may think that we are following God, but we are not. We cannot follow God a little in one thing and follow Buddha a little in something else, for then we are not following God at all. We cannot honour God with our words without honouring God with our money and possessions, for then whatever we say with our lips is rendered worthless and even dishonouring to God.

The southern kingdom, Judah, thought she was better than the northern kingdom of Israel for at least she partially followed God, but there is no such thing as partially following God. It is all or nothing. Israel was more open in her sin and therefore God spoke of her as in some ways more right – because she did not defame God by sinning and claiming to do so in his name; she merely sinned.[242] Judah saw the sin of Israel and should have learnt from it, but instead she did worse.[243] Unless our whole lives are dedicated to God, we will inevitably end up worshipping a false god in some aspect of our life.

PRIDE, SELF-SUFFICIENCY, AND TRUSTING IN PAGAN NATIONS

The Israelites were proud in their wealth and gladly showed it off in good clothing and much jewellery.[244] They pursued lives of pleasures and self-interest.[245] They gloried in their wealth when they should have gloried in God.[246]

They thought that they were wise, but in fact they had exchanged truth for lies, good for evil, light for darkness, sweet for bitter.[247] They thought that they were more holy, when in fact they were less so.[248] So easily do we become captured by the way that the world thinks, which is to worship individualism, wealth, and the pursuit of self-interest. We think that we are doing what is right – in the western world, pursuing self-interest and financial security – when in fact we are often doing very wrong.

As part of their harlotry, the Israelites trusted in the strength of man and taking strength from people rather than from God.[249] They looked to foreign nations like Assyria for protection and provision rather than to God, and repeatedly sent tribute to foreign nations.[250] They thought that all their good things – food and water, wool and linen, oil and drink – came from these foreign powers rather than from God.[251] They rejected God and the cisterns he had provided for foreign nations and their broken cisterns that could not hold water.[252] They failed to see that it was God who had taught them, as a nation, to walk and who had healed, guided, and fed them.[253]

God showed the Israelites the way to live, but they chose the way of the peoples around them – the way of trusting in the strength of man, in their own wisdom and abilities, in following false gods. They rejected trust in God for trust in wealth and power, looking to the resources God had given them to protect themselves yet failing to look to God himself.[254] God controlled the sea – an image of power and evil – and he ordained the seasons and the harvest, yet the people did not trust him for protection and provision.[255] Instead, they trusted in their own strength[256] and that of the nations around them.

Even after returning from exile, God's people failed to trust and obey him. In Haggai, the complaint was that the people were not benefiting as much as they expected from their work.[257] The reason was that God was frustrating their work because they were not honouring him.[258] They were striving for their own gain whilst the house of God was in ruins. They sought their own wealth but did not seek God's glory nor honour him. Consequently, because of their sin, everything that they did – including what they did offer to God – was defiled.[259]

Obadiah continues the same message against the Edomites. The Edomites were the descendants of Jacob's elder brother, Esau. Edom had, like Israel, failed to acknowledge God's sovereignty and instead trusted in her own strength and impregnability.[260] Not only that, but Edom had failed to defend Israel when she was under attack and had even mocked her, plundered her, and assisted her victors to oppress her.[261] God's judgment against her was to reverse her fortunes: where once she had been proud, now Edom would be despised.[262]

God's requirement that we acknowledge and worship him, trust ourselves to him alone, and defend and care for the poor applies to all nations, not just to a theocracy or an Israelite or Christian nation. It is not acceptable that we use the world's ways of pursuing security. We are not to seek after money and position as though those things will protect us; we are not to join in the world's self-centred behaviour, as though we cannot afford to be just or generous. We are called to trust God's provision for us, and live according to his ways.

SEXUAL IMMORALITY

Although it is not as dominant a theme as oppressive behaviours and religious adultery, the Israelites were also guilty of personal sexual immorality.[263] This included adultery and visiting prostitutes. God even said that he would not punish the women for prostitution and adultery, for the men were no better.[264] At other times, personal sexual immorality occurred in concert with idolatry, as pagan rites often included sexual acts.[265] Father and son would sleep with the same woman (possibly a temple prostitute, as part of fertility rites) and then lie down to eat before pagan altars, lying on clothes that they had taken in pledge from the poor, drinking wine that they had taken as fines. Thus they combined adultery, idolatry, greed, theft, and oppression in one night.[266]

The relative infrequency of rebuke for personal sexual immorality cannot be because this behaviour is unimportant to God, as otherwise it would not make sense for God to use sexual immorality as a metaphor for the Israelites' behaviour towards him. It seems rather that, in the range of sins committed, this was a less common one than sins of idolatry and injustice. Nevertheless, when it did occur it was a serious sin.

We are to take sexual sin seriously in our lives. However, sexual purity is not the sole requirement of God outside of religious rites. In the Western world, we may need to take care not to neglect the other sins in which we engage, or ignore the importance of idolatry and injustice in the way we live.

THE ROLE OF INDIVIDUALS

The Israelites were guilty of many sins before God even as they thought that they were holy, protected, and faithful. They were so ignorant of their own sin that when true prophets warned them, they rejected the prophets. God challenged the Israelites for forsaking him, even as they continued with the outward appearance of religion; for trusting in power, wealth, and foreign nations and gods instead of him; for acting oppressively and unjustly, and so creating and maintaining poverty and injustice; and for engaging in sexual immorality, often in connection with pagan rituals.

Across the prophets, we see that God is concerned with the whole of our lives. It is not just how we perform the religious rituals or the individual, private acts of our lives, but also the public acts and the ways in which how we choose to live impact upon other people. God expects us to show the same love and faithfulness that he shows us to both him and all people, especially the poor. He expects us to act with love, justice, and a particular concern for those who are in need and are being harmed by those with more power and wealth.

Consumers

One of the biggest ways in which we can do this is in our roles as consumers. It is well-established that Western lifestyles massively over-consume the earth's resources. If we factored in the depletion of earth's resources, there would be no such thing as economic growth; all we would have achieved so far would be massive economic destruction.[267] If everyone lived as the average UK resident lives, we would need another earth and a half to support us all; if everyone lived as the average USA resident lives, we would need five earths.[268] God gave us dominion over the earth, but not to destroy it through selfish, heedless living. He gave us dominion in order to tame, nurture, and care for nature. We simply don't have any right to over-consume, and we should not do so.

In many ways we should simply reduce our purchase of goods. It is easy to think that by donating unwanted clothes or other items to charity, we are doing a good thing. But actually, if our clothes still have a wearable life in them, we should continue to wear them, and not replace them with other clothes. The purchase of unnecessary clothes is part of our over-consumption of the earth. Many unwanted clothes go to Majority World (MW) countries where they swamp out local clothes producers, hamper the MW economy, and use up air miles.

Our expectation that anything we might want should always be in stock means that suppliers have to over-stock, and then end up with waste product that is unsold and thrown out. This applies as much to food and other consumables as it does to clothes. When the combined impacts of Brexit, COVID-19, and global supply chain disruptions resulted in shortages of some goods in some parts of the UK, there were many complaints. And yet no-one went hungry as a result of some goods being out of stock; they merely had to wait a few days or purchase a different item. Our consumer-driven mentality can't cope with the idea that husbanding the earth's resources means not having everything we want on hand immediately all of the time. Sometimes we should just go without. We should learn to live with knowing that we cannot always get exactly what we want, but as long as there is something to meet our needs we can do just fine.

In other situations, we should reduce the size of what

we buy. If we need a car – because public transport and/or Shanks's pony is inadequate (and we should think seriously about whether this is the case, or are we just accustomed to the ease of middle-class living?) – then we should buy the smallest, most environmentally friendly car we can. Many 'luxury' or 'business' cars are unfit for purpose; they are like a reverse TARDIS, smaller on the inside than their footprint could afford.

My twin sister is married, and she and her husband share one car. Her husband cycles 45 minutes to work, even in the rain. They recognise that their lives would be 'easier' if they had two cars, but they consider that an extravagance too far. They don't 'need' two cars by any standard that includes responsibility for the earth's resources; they only 'need' two cars in order to meet middle class living standards, and there is no biblical justification for such a style of living. Nor do they have a particularly large car, even though at times their car is cramped with three adults, two young children, and all the paraphernalia that comes with babies and toddlers.

Thinking carefully about how much we purchase and consume, and the most environmentally friendly versions of what we need, is one way in which our lives can bring glory to God rather than blaspheme him. It tells people that we care about God's creation and take seriously our responsibility for it. It demonstrates to Christians and non-Christians alike that what God meant by 'subdue' and 'have dominion over' was not rape and pillage, but to use the earth for human good whilst yet walking amongst the animals more as a ruler who chooses to act as an equal than as extractive oppressors. This is, after all, how God walks amongst us.

It is not at all difficult to do. It is easy to find second-hand cars for sale, and these are cheaper than new cars; it is easy to purchase clothes from charity shops or from organic and ethical manufacturers, and charity shops are cheap; it is easy to buy organic and grass-fed meat, and to reduce our meat consumption in order to afford more ethical meat when we do eat it; it is easy to find household and hygiene products that are better for the earth, like reusable sanitary towels for women or cleaning products in concentrated form. It is not difficult to choose more ethical and environmentally friendly options or to simply reduce consumption; and when we reduce consumption, we free up money that can be used to directly help other people. We might make mistakes; we might find that what we thought was the environmentally friendly option has its own problems. But we can learn from those mistakes, whereas if we don't try at all then we will never live gently on Earth.

Security

Both the Israelites and pagan countries placed their trust in one another and their own wealth and power to save them rather than looking to God.[269] Many leaders and nations sought to raise themselves up in power and glory; to be at the very top and rule like a god.[270] They failed to listen to God and instead listened to the foolish and senseless advice of the world, which is like trusting in astrologers and stargazers.[271] In the current time this is like listening to the advice of money-makers and the ultra-rich as though money (particularly money at the top) and economic growth (without consideration for its distribution or the impact on the earth) is what matters most, or as though these people know the most about what is important in human life.

It is very easy to look to the wrong things for security. In general, I think we are often unaware of what we place our security in until that thing is removed. We may place our security in our job and assume that the regular income will provide for us and our families. But those jobs can be taken away by ill-health, redundancy, or a pandemic, leaving us unable to earn enough to support ourselves. Or sudden extra costs may fall on us, like the need to remove unsafe external cladding from buildings and the arguments over who is paying, or an allegation made against us which we have to defend in court at high cost. Even if we have thousands of pounds stashed in a bank account, such money can be stolen, or a bank can collapse. We can't trust in money to look after us, because money cannot guarantee to always be there when we need it or be adequate to meet unexpected needs. Yet we very easily do so, fretting about whether we have enough savings, earn enough money, or have taken out enough insurance to look after us rather than genuinely trusting God to look after us.

A simple example that many of us may not even think about is when we go to buy a car. Some people choose a new car over second-hand for fear that an older car is more likely to break down, and they think that they need the security of a reliable car. Or at least, that's how they justify spending large amounts on an environmentally-destructive option. But should you place your trust in the newness of your material possessions rather than in God? Could you save money by instead buying a substantially cheaper car (cars lose a lot of value in the first few years) but getting breakdown insurance? Are there other strategies you could use, like being aware of the public transport options and regularly using a bicycle, both so that your car gets less use (so lasts longer) and so you are more used to cycling and it isn't such a hardship if it becomes a necessity? Why choose the perception of security rather than the option that frees up what God has given you to bless others?

We may find ourselves trusting in our position of influence. Jesus told a parable about a financial manager who used his influence to buy friends for himself, so that when he was in need he would be cared for.[272] Jesus' command to us is not that we seek to make contacts who will help us, but that we use what we have to buy security in the Kingdom of Heaven. We should not be deliberately making connections with people who have power or influence in order to be confident of a soft landing if anything ever goes wrong with our current job. Instead, we should be seeking to make connections with people who need what we have. We should continually be using our resources not to make connections with people above us in power and influence, but with people below us; using our resources not to help ourselves, but to help others. Our spare time should not be spent learning to play golf so that we can keep up with the bigwigs, but in learning to serve those in need. This is what buys us the friendship in heaven that truly sees us through life's difficulties. The apostle Paul says the same kind of thing when he says that we should not steal and grab things to ourselves, but should work with our hands so that we have something to share with those in need.[273]

The only security we should pursue is that offered by Jesus. He doesn't promise to protect our wealth or position on earth, but instead to protect our wealth and position in heaven. He promises to see us through to salvation and eternity with him, including rewards for our behaviour on earth. He doesn't guarantee us a home every night, but he does guarantee a home in the new heavens and earth. He doesn't say he will keep us free of all sickness and disease on earth, but he does say that there will be no suffering or disability when he restores all things.

Pursuing wealth, power, and people of wealth and power on earth takes our time and effort. God says that it is a wrong use of our energies and a poor return on our effort. Instead, we should put our time and effort into helping others, and in that way we invest in the kingdom of heaven. Instead of saving up money for our future selves, we should use that money to help others now, and thereby save in the bank of heaven.

Business

Economists have a term, 'rent-seeking', for a certain kind of stealing that many people in developed countries engage in without even realising that what they are doing is theft. Rent-seeking is when a person who owns something that someone else needs – perhaps a house, or farmland, or equipment for making goods for sale – charges that other person merely to have access to it. A fee that covers the administration time or maintenance costs is not rent-seeking; rather, rent-seeking refers to that extra money which is pure profit merely because the owner has something that someone else needs. It is grabbing more money to yourself purely because you already have money (or tangible assets), and therefore have the power to do so. A typical example of rent-seeking is when landlords charge rent at a level that brings them income after administration, insurance, and maintenance.

Another kind of theft, but less direct, is when a person or business does not pay to remedy the pollution or other harm they cause. Again, this is often an indirect consequence of pursuing money as the aim of a business or goal of our lives rather than seeing our purpose on earth as being to glorify God by serving others. Nicholas Townsend points out that business should be about providing goods and services, and the quality of what we provide, and not primarily about making profit. 'In neoliberal capitalism, ends and means have been mistaken for each other.'[274]

Townsend also writes that 'in the aftermath of the 2008 financial crisis, the need to draw on the wealth of resources in Scripture and the Christian tradition that address the basic moral issues in this area is overwhelming. The first thing to be said is that these are moral issues. There has been no deeper cause of the economic crisis than the explicit denial in the neoliberal capitalism which has dominated recent decades that what people do in markets should be subject to moral analysis.'[275]

With money as the security for our business, practices that God would condemn become common sense that of course we follow. We justify this wickedness to ourselves because we say that it is better that we run a (moderately harmful) business than that we run no business at all (and let businesses that are 'even more' harmful thrive in our place). But God does not accept such self-justifying excuses. He calls them wicked. When we impose costs upon other people – when we don't pay labourers enough for their work; or over-charge customers; or pollute someone else's land or air – then we are stealing from them. And that is not okay, even if we think that we are better for our employees, customers, and neighbours because we don't steal as much from them as our competitor does. God does not permit this kind of wicked justification of abusive practices. God commands us to do what is right, and he will deal with those who do what is wrong.

If you are a business owner, then as a Christian you must ensure that all of your staff – including the often out-sourced cleaners and so-on – have enough pay to live off decently, are not pressurised to work at high speed, and generally have decent and enjoyable working conditions. This may well include no zero-hours contracts, but instead a number and distribution of hours that meet what the worker needs and will benefit from, and what is also good for his or her family. Unless necessary, as in care and emergency work, workers should not be required or expected to work overnight, because this damages health by disrupting the circadian rhythms. 'Consumers' may want convenience, but 'workers' are consumers and people too. Work should be set according to what is good for the worker, not what is good for the employer; trust should be in God, not in predatory business practices.

CONCLUSION

As Christians, we have to think about how every part of our life affects other people. We are to do what is right, even if we think that the consequence may be negative. Jonah, after all, did not want to go to Nineveh because he feared the consequences of God not passing punishment on them. And he was right: some decades later, Assyria invaded Israel and conquered her. Had God carried out his judgment on Assyria, she might not later have been in a position to conquer Israel. But this did not mean that it was wrong for God to give Assyria the opportunity to repent, or wrong for Jonah to preach that repentance. Instead, it would have been wrong to not give Assyria such an opportunity. The fear of negative consequences should not be an excuse for not doing what God says is right. We must think about how we live on this earth, to make sure that we are not over-consuming, damaging the environment, or relying on exploited people to serve us.

CHAPTER 7

THE SIN OF THE LEADERS

JESUS TOLD THE PHARISEES, the chief priests, and the elders of the people that the tax collectors and prostitutes would get into heaven in front of them. This was shocking. These were the people charged with knowing the word and will of God, looked up to for leadership by the general public. And Jesus said that people who engaged in some of the worst sins, and betrayed and impoverished their own people, were better than those who earnestly pursued God.

One argument is that the prostitutes and tax collectors were welcome because they were oppressed and outcast from society. Although they engaged in sin, they suffered from it in the rejection they experienced from otherwise 'respectable' people. In welcoming them, Jesus was reversing the rejection that society showed. He was coming out on the side of the unwanted and despised.

This, however, is not quite the story that Jesus tells. Jesus tells a parable of a man who had two sons.[276] He asks his first son to go and work in the vineyard. The son says he will go, but then doesn't. The father asks his second son to work, and this son says he won't work but then changes his mind and does go to work.

When Jesus asks which son obeyed his father, the answer is obvious: the second son. The second son started off as disobedient but then repented and obeyed. The first son said he would be obedient, but then was disobedient. The parallel that Jesus was making was that the prostitutes and tax collectors who would enter the Kingdom of Heaven ahead of the Jewish leaders were like the second son: they had disobeyed, but had since repented. It was their repentance, not their oppressed or outcast status, that got them into heaven. Meanwhile those people who claimed to obey but did not do so in practice were lagging behind. There was still time to repent, but they had not done so yet, even though they thought they were superior to the (ex) tax collectors and prostitutes.

The tying together of prostitute and tax collector is challenging if we think that we have to make the tax collector into an oppressed person in order to make him welcome to Jesus. But the truth is that the tax collectors were oppressors who had betrayed and exploited their own people for their own financial gain. We have two opposite people groups: sinful, probably oppressed, women; and sinful, oppressive, men. Jesus is saying something more radical than that the outcasts of society are accepted by him. He is saying that the oppressors are accepted too; that he loves and yearns for them; that he welcomes all who repent, regardless of what they had to repent of.

The radical message of God is that it doesn't matter who we are: outcast or insider; oppressed or oppressor; recognised sinners or arrogant 'saints'. We all need to repent of our sin; and we are all accepted by him, through the death and resurrection of Jesus, if we do place our trust in him. And to know what we need to repent of – what actions we must turn from, and what we must start to do – we need to know what God has revealed of himself through his word. We need to know how we are to live and how we are to relate to one another.

OPPRESSION

After rejection of God and allegiance to false gods, oppression is the next most dominant theme in the prophets' message to the Israelites. It is raised nearly 100 times by Isaiah, Jeremiah and Ezekiel. It is a source of major concern and anger to God, who tells his people that unless they administer justice and rescue the oppressed, his 'wrath will break out and burn like fire because of the evil you have done – burn with no one to quench it.'[277] Both rejection of God and allegiance to false gods are related to oppression: failing to act justly and generously is de facto a rejection of God and his Word; and allegiance to the false gods of wealth and power is necessarily and inextricably linked with injustice. Several of the minor prophets make injustice and oppression a major theme of their message, and it is inextricably interwoven into many of God's indictments against his people.

Amos

Amos is a treatise against injustice and oppression. It is not just directed at Israel; God also accused pagan nations of injustice and oppression in their treatment of other nations. He described them as threshing other nations with iron teeth; taking whole communities captive and selling them into slavery; pursuing foreign peoples with the sword; ripping open pregnant women; and burning the bones of a foreign king.[278] But his condemnation of Israel and Judah was much more detailed: Judah had rejected God's law and followed false gods;[279] and Israel had sold the righteous and the needy for money; trampled the poor into the ground; refused justice to the oppressed; slept with prostitutes; and used garments taken as pledge and wine taken as fines to worship false gods.[280]

The women were just as bad, combining their lust for drink with oppression of the poor, and earning themselves the name 'cows of Bashan', after the well-fed cows that came from that region.[281] Amos later described the lifestyles of the rich: they built mansions and 'lush vineyards'; lay on beds inlaid with ivory; ate the very finest lambs and fattest calves; made up meaningless, idle songs; drank wine by the bowlful; and used the finest of lotions.[282] All of these are spoken of as unacceptable. Whether because these lifestyles were obtained by unjust practices, or maintained by lack of charitable generosity, it was unacceptable to God.

The well-off stole not just clothes and wine from those in need of help, but the very grain that the poor of the land had worked to grow and harvest.[283] Because the rich had not let the poor and the workers enjoy the fruit of the work, and instead had siphoned off the profit to themselves, God would remove from them even the houses and vineyards to which they did contribute.[284] The excesses of both sexes' behaviour was denounced alongside injustice and oppression, tying the two together.

The Israelites had turned 'justice into bitterness, and cast righteousness to the ground'.[285] They hated those who spoke the truth, and they took bribes and would 'deprive the poor of justice in the courts'.[286] Compounding their silencing of those who challenged them, the better-off told God's prophets to speak lies in God's name and to tell the people to break their vows.[287] The rich not only unjustly deprived the poor of what they had worked for and ungenerously denied support to the poor, but they also objected when the poor and the prophets denounced their bad behaviour.

Micah

Micah describes how the Israelites had been deeply unjust in their personal and business lives. They found ways to take other people's fields, houses, and inheritance;[288] they took clothing without any care for the victim and drove women out of their homes;[289] and they so oppressed, exploited, and stole from the poor that God called it cannibalism.[290] The pursuit of wealth in this way, with no concern for the loss experienced by the other, is a form of theft when it leaves people without what they need to survive, defend themselves, and participate in society.[291] Worse than that: this acquisition of wealth is akin to tearing off poor people's skin and flesh, breaking up their bones, and cutting them up as meat for the table.[292] We might just as well eat the poor as accumulate wealth for ourselves; our injustice is the same as deliberate killing.[293] To deprive people of decent shelter and the means to live is a terrible sin.

God's complaint against Israel and Judah was not only that they had committed such a wide range of unjust and oppressive acts, but that they had done so despite being his chosen nation. He himself had rescued the Israelites from Egypt, led them through the desert, and given them prophets to teach them of him, yet they had rejected him.[294] They had been oppressed and rescued from oppression, yet they had become oppressors themselves. They had been given a land by God's grace, not by deservingness, yet they were not living lives that showed grace towards one another. God even gave his people warnings of his coming judgement, yet they did not listen to his discipline.[295]

Nahum and Jonah

The books of Nahum and Jonah are directed against the foreign nation, Assyria, whose capital was Nineveh. Nineveh had produced people who plotted evil against God and advised others in wickedness.[296] She followed false gods[297] and enslaved other nations and peoples through her prostitution and witchcraft.[298] Nahum described her as a 'city of blood, full of lies, full of plunder, never without victims'.[299] Her merchants were like locusts: they stripped the land bare, then left without any care for the people they had plundered.[300] This language of blood, lies, and harlotry is similar to the language used against the Israelites to describe economic injustice, idolatry, and reliance on powerful nations rather than God for protection. In Nahum, God showed that pagan nations will also be judged for their economic oppression and their trust in false gods, power, and wealth.

In Jonah, we are not told what Nineveh's sin is. What the book of Jonah tells us is both that God does care about how non-believers and non-theocratic nations behave; and that if a nation changes its ways, God relents from sending punishment. And nations can change their ways, especially when challenged by a prophet about their sin.

Habakkuk

The book of Habakkuk is another treatise on injustice. The prophet Habakkuk complained of destruction, violence, strife, and conflict that paralysed the law and prevented and perverted justice amongst the Israelites.[301] God answered that he would raise up the Babylonians to judge Israel for her sin.

Habakkuk's next concern was that the Babylonians were so ruthless that Israel would be utterly destroyed.[302] Babylon was a nation even more corrupt than Israel, plundering other nations like a trawlerman plundering the sea. She acted like a fisherman who keeps pulling more and more fish out of the sea, selling her catch to gain luxuries for herself, ever greedy for more. Yet men are not fish to be exploited without any thought for their wellbeing.

Babylon was arrogant, praising her net – her business capital and practices – for the wealth she accrued.[303] Yet the net, like an idol, was of no use for security for it is made by men.[304] It is God who created and sustained the fish, not man; it is God who gives men the strength to work and who made the resources that we use. We are never to use what God has given us as a source of pride in ourselves; and we are never to use it to oppress rather than help others.

God acknowledged to Habakkuk that Babylon was proud, greedy, and corrupt.[305] Eventually Babylon also would be judged and then it would be a time of woe for all the evil people within her: those who piled up stolen goods; plundered nations; grew wealthy through crime, extortion, and unjust practices; destroyed land and buildings; killed the people; and made others drunk in order to laugh at them.[306] The accumulation of wealth by the rich was a theft and exploitation of the poor that was akin to murder, compounded by deliberately exposing people in order to mock them.

God promised that a time would come when Babylon and her better-off citizens would suffer what they had imposed upon others. As they had stolen and exploited and lived in excess, so they would in turn be plundered and exposed to disgrace. The grasping, selfish, exploitative mindset of the Babylonians is not acceptable to God.

Zechariah

Zechariah started his prophecy with a call to Judah to take note of the exile inflicted upon her ancestors, and to learn from this and repent.[307] Their oppression of the widow, fatherless, foreigner, and poor – people who lacked a defender – was an offense to God which made him very angry.[308] God had graciously sent multiple prophets to declare his full word to them, but the previous Israelites had ignored the prophets.[309] In the end, God's sinful people were sent into exile, and God refused to listen to them just as they had refused to listen to those whom they were meant to protect.[310] We must not repeat the same mistake of refusing to listen to those in need.

When the previous generations had fasted and mourned, they had not truly done so for God's sake rather than their own. Their lack of true justice, mercy, and compassion meant that their humility was false even as they thought they were genuine.[311] God called upon them to cease their lies, administer true justice, and live to help rather than harm their neighbours.[312] When their actions matched their words, that would be true humility before God.

The major prophets

The Israelites continued to bring offerings to God throughout their time in the land of Israel. But their offerings were meaningless because of their evil deeds and wrongdoing by failing to maintain justice or defend the defenceless and oppressed.[313] Justice for Israel did not mean being set free from oppressors (foreign nations that subdued Israel), but being disciplined for being the oppressor. Israel thought that the enactment of full justice would mean that she could rejoice; in fact, it would mean weeping and sorrow as she was disciplined for her wickedness.

God's people were all 'greedy for gain'[314] and God called this accumulation of wealth 'crushing my people and grinding the faces of the poor'.[315] It was the possessions of the poor that filled the houses of the rich,[316] because everything ultimately belongs to God. It is not part of his plans for humanity that some should have more than they need whilst others do not have enough. As God said to Shallum, King of Judah, 'Does it make you a king to have more and more cedar? Did not your father have food and drink? He did what was right and just, and so all went well with him. He defended the cause of the poor and needy, and so all went well. Is that not what it means to know me?'.[317] But the Israelites rejected the messages that God's prophets brought them about how to truly follow God, and instead continued to use oppression and deceit for their own gain.[318]

In Ezekiel 34, God condemned the rich Israelites for bullying and oppressing the poor.[319] These weren't the leaders, whom God compared to bad shepherds, but rich citizens whose lifestyles harmed the poorer people in society. God complained of them that they were not just taking more than they needed for themselves (and so had become fat) but were preventing the poor from meeting their own needs. He compared rich people to fat sheep who drove away thin sheep, trampled the grass, and muddied the water. God said that when he judged between shepherd and sheep, he would also judge between fat sheep and thin sheep. He would save the thin sheep and be to them the good shepherd, driving off the bullying and oppressive fat sheep and worthless shepherds.

There is a suggestion in Isaiah that the better-off Israelites had been doing what the UK and many developed countries do: slander the poor as a reason to not provide help. We say that they will spend it on drugs, or that it will encourage feckless behaviour; we say that what is really needed is 'tough love' that allows people to suffer the consequences of failing to secure a permanent, full-time, decently paid job. But God calls this 'devising wicked schemes' in order to 'destroy the needy with slander'.[320] He says that people who talk and act like this are rogues. He says that those who do not feed the hungry or give water to the thirsty are wicked and ungodly fools who 'speak error against the LORD'.[321]

How easily do we do the same things? We have laws that allow people to profit off other people's poverty, charging interest on loans for essential living costs and charging rent to access the basic necessity of a home. We use loopholes and clever money-shuffling to avoid paying tax, and find excuses to justify our standard of living whilst others are suffering. The appearance of legality is not the same as morality before God, and we must be careful not to kid ourselves about the acceptability of our lifestyles.

What God wants is for us to work for an end to injustice, freedom for the oppressed, and provision for those in need.[322] God wants a reformation of our ways and actions, which he explains as meaning that we deal with each other justly, do not oppress the defenceless, and do not shed innocent blood.[323] This use of 'bloodshed' is a metaphor used by God to refer to all kinds of oppression. According to God, to deprive someone of what God has provided for their needs is not just theft, but akin to murder. Not everyone will die immediately for lack of what they need, but people not only suffer whilst they live but die before their time because we have not ensured that their need is met out of our riches. Failing to do this – to do what is just and right; rescue the oppressed and robbed; protect the defenceless; cause no bloodshed – is to forsake our covenant with God.[324]

God was also concerned for his Sabbath day to be kept holy. In Jeremiah 17:21-27, God's call is for his people to remember the Sabbath day and keep it holy. In Isaiah 56, the command is 'maintain justice and do what is right' with a blessing for 'the man who does this, the man who holds it fast, who keeps the Sabbath without desecrating it and keeps his hand from doing any evil'.[325] Part of the holiness of God's Sabbath day is the execution of justice across the land; part of justice is the right protection of the Sabbath for all people. There is no Sabbath day that exists only for the better-off to rest and relax whilst the poor continue to labour. That is just as much a mockery of God as the offerings that the Israelites brought.

It is no use to have the right words but no actions; to speak peace yet live lives that foster oppression and injustice.[326] Too often we say nice things to our neighbours, but our lives are ones of oppression and deceit.[327] God does not want the fat off our riches. He had no use for frankincense from Sheba[328] and nor does he want a tithe of ill-gotten gains. Our sacrifices and offerings to him are unacceptable if they are made from a heart that is greedy and unjust, or out of wealth that we should not have had.[329]

The sacrifices that the Israelites continued to offer were nothing to God if his people did not act justly, love mercy, and walk humbly with God.[330]

God does not want the rituals of religion if they are not accompanied by holy and righteous behaviour in our private and public lives.[331] When we try to follow God's religious rites at the same time as failing to meet the needs of the poor or to defend the oppressed against their oppressors, we turn our religion into nothing more than a superstitious rite; the buying of God's favour through gifts whilst not otherwise aligning our lives with his. This made sense for the pagan gods, who were capricious and not worthy of obedience (not least because they didn't exist, so couldn't reliably respond to sacrifices). But our God is not a pagan god. He is the one true God, who can only be worshipped in spirit and truth, not through rites and superstition.

God wants the circumcision of our hearts, but the Israelites trusted in their circumcision of the flesh and failed to see that their lives were meant to be lived in accordance with that.[332]

BLOODSHED

More than 30 verses in the books of the prophets refer to injustice as bloodshed. The most common use of the language of blood and bloodshed is in this context of oppression. Ezekiel uses the word 'blood' and its derivatives eight times in a single chapter, chapter 22. Every leader of Israel, God said, has used his power to shed blood through this behaviour:

'In you they have treated father and mother with contempt; in you they have oppressed the foreigner and mistreated the fatherless and the widow... in you are slanderous men… in you men accept bribes … you take usury and interest and make unjust gains from your neighbours by extortion … they devour people, take treasures and precious things and make many widows within her … the people of the land practise extortion and commit robbery; they oppress the poor and needy and ill-treat the alien, denying them justice.'[333]

'In you they have treated father and mother with contempt'

The Israelites had not cared for their aged parents, but had refused to provide for them in their need. It was a command of God that people honour their parents,[334] and the sentence for cursing one's parents was death.[335] The Israelite justice system was based on the principle of like for like. So in stipulating that the sentence for cursing one's parents was death, God was likening the intention or effect of a curse to murder.

Curses were more than a wish for bad things to fall upon a person; they were considered to have power through the agency of God or gods to bring about that bad thing. Later biblical texts expanded upon the understanding of curses, clarifying that they had no effect where there was no just cause for the curse[336] but apportioning the same judgment to the speaker of the curse whether it was spoken internally or out loud, without intention or with deliberate intention to harm.[337] God judges the attitude, not merely the consequence. If a person's attitude is one of harm towards others, God judges as though that harm has occurred.

In God's eyes, lack of care is as bad as deliberate harm. This applies as much today to individuals in western countries and to western countries themselves as it did to

Israelites and Israel. God does not cease to care about the harm we cause one another just because we do not live in a theocratic nation. One of the key duties that we have is to care for our relatives, in particular parents or children, when they are in need of help. Yet in many Western countries, we emphasise individualism over community. We expect to be able to move around the country and even the world for work or for what pleases us, without thought for what that means for the family we leave behind. Perhaps our ageing parents need someone to make sure that any social care they receive is adequate, whilst also making sure that they do indeed receive 'social' support and not just personal care. Perhaps one of our siblings needs help with childcare. Perhaps our own children need help as adults. Yet we cannot support our families if we live many miles away.

This is also a matter for our government. God was speaking directly to the leaders of the Israelites when he accused them of treating father and mother with contempt. Perhaps he was speaking simply of the parents of the leaders; but he may also have been speaking of the type of society that the leaders oversaw, which was one that resulted in contempt for parents. For example, in the UK many poor people are forced to move away from their parents in order to receive a social house. In this way, the government forces poor people to treat their parents with contempt, by preventing the poor from maintaining a family life and contributing to the care of elderly parents. Our society is also one that mocks the working class for valuing community and living near family over moving for a better job.

'In you they have oppressed the foreigner'

God has always been strong on the necessity that his people care for those who are not his people. Israel was the collection of his chosen people into his chosen nation. The foreigner was therefore any non-Israelite. God's command to Israel, as his people and his country, was this: 'When an alien lives in your land, do not ill-treat him. The alien living with you must be treated as one of your native-born. Love him as yourself, for you were aliens in Egypt. I am the Lord your God.'[338]

Some commenters say that the foreigners in view here were non-Israelites who had chosen to enter the Israelite community and followed Israelite religion including circumcision, sacrifices, and cleanliness laws. But the point made here is that the Israelites had themselves been strangers in Egypt, and they had not at that time assimilated into Egyptian religion and culture. God loves all people, whatever people group or culture they are from.

The command for the Israelites was that, in looking back to their time in Egypt when they were enslaved, they should choose to act towards foreigners in their own country as God had acted towards them when they were in Egypt, and not as Pharaoh had acted towards them. The same principle remains true for Christians today: we should behave like God, not like Pharaoh or the common ways of mankind. Just as the Israelites looked back to a time when they were enslaved in Egypt, we look back to when we were enslaved to sin, and are to be encouraged by this to help the stranger.

Our government must also have thought for the needs of foreigners. It should not be acceptable, for example, to deliberately pay a foreigner less than a UK citizen would receive for a given job. Pragmatically speaking, there are costs to the home nation when many of their strongest and brightest people leave, and there is an impact on the families left behind as well. It may be appropriate to consider other ways in which the UK can support people of other nations, such as through exchange programmes, or through international aid to help poorer countries to develop, that do not harm foreign countries or break up families. More fundamentally, we should not exploit poorer countries for our own gain, and we should consider how our actions – such as in polluting the environment – cause harm to other nations.

'In you they have ... ill-treated the fatherless and the widow'

God has always had a special consideration for those who are defenceless and unprovided for. This was typified for Israel by children with no parents (or at least no father), women who had lost their husbands, and foreigners (who likely had no local family). Other people groups listed by God as to be protected and provided for include those who are generally poor, and those who are needy or sick. The claim that these people made upon the better-off Israelites was not a claim of family, because the point here is that these are people without immediate family, but a claim of need. In Israel, the neighbour whom you helped was not to be merely your family, friends, or 'family in faith', but whoever was in need.

The leaders of Israel had a responsibility to protect and provide for the poor and needy, but instead had pursued policies that caused ill-treatment. Our governments must also act to care for those in need, and not enact policies that bring harm to these people. Like in Israel, this is likely to mean proactive legislation that provides for the needs of people in poverty and ensures that they can maintain status in society.

'You have despised my holy things and desecrated my Sabbaths'

God condemned his people for their improper use of fasting. Instead of using it to repent truly and draw closer to God, they defiled it by divorcing their economic and social lives from their religious lives. So they continued to oppress and exploit their workers even on a day of fasting when the day of fasting should have been an opportunity to reflect on one's treatment of one's workers and how to improve their wellbeing. There was therefore no true repentance amongst the fasting Israelites because they did not consider their social and economic actions to be of relevance to their religion.

When our economic and social actions do not match our religious claims, then we dishonour God and despise his holy things. We defile his holiness with our dirtiness. It is a dirtiness that cannot be washed off without true repentance and a change in action. Remorse is not what God is looking for, nor a Catholic indulgence; no claim of being sorry when we do not change course is acceptable to God. Our sin in our social and economic lives is like bringing money changers and cheats into the temple of God. We defile his temple, block people from accessing God, and misrepresent God to those who most need his help.

Instead, God says, we are to do away with the yoke of oppression, with the pointing finger and malicious talk; we are to spend ourselves on behalf of the hungry and satisfy the needs of the oppressed.[339] Our governments must also ensure that people are not oppressed, including ensuring sufficient provision for rest and personal life, in a manner similar to that provided for by God through the Sabbath. Governments must also respect religion and not despise the reasonable beliefs of those who adhere to a religion.

'In you men accept bribes to take blood'

'Accepting bribes to take blood' probably doesn't refer to paid assassins taking out an enemy or opponent. God uses blood as a metaphor for oppression because oppressing people is like physically harming or even killing them. God takes it that seriously. So here we have leaders who 'sell-out'. They take a bribe from big business and agree to look the other way when that business worsens its working conditions or reduces its pay for its frontline workers. They accept donations from the wealthy and in return listen to what they want on policy matters. They live, work, and socialise amongst the rich – the opposite of Jesus' command to his disciples in Luke 14 – and so fill their minds with the ideas of the rich. Without realising it, their thoughts are captured by what the rich want, and they sell out the poor. They are bought by the rich, and the consequence is suffering, injustice, unhappy lives, and early deaths.

A classic example is seen in Yanis Varoufakis' book *Adults in the Room*, as he describes how Greek politicians sold out their people to the wishes of the European elite. Another can be seen in the UK government's response to the fatal fire in the Grenfell tower block, as politicians continue to dither and fail to ensure that either the government or the original providers of dangerous cladding pay for the removal and replacement of this cladding. The same issue is present in the rhetoric around the lives of the poor, with government failing to understand the structural causes of poverty which they and previous governments have caused through their policies.

The things that matter and are priorities to the rich are different from what matters to the poor, but it is the poor whose needs should be prioritised.

'You take usury and excessive interest'

God was very clear that his people were to be generous to those in need. This was not merely an issue of charity, but a question of justice. The cancellation of debt every seventh year was in essence a command that where someone could not repay a loan, they were to be given what they needed instead. The ban on any form of interest is so unfamiliar to western readers that translators translate into 'excessive interest' a word that simply means 'interest'. But in God's economy, lending is never about making money for the lender but about helping, even giving to, the borrower. It is about the borrower's needs even at cost to the lender.

Profiting from another person's poverty is abhorrent to God. There is no place for interest-bearing loans for living costs in a decent country. If a person does not have enough to meet their basic costs, then they should be given what they need. The presence of pay-day loans, loan sharks, and any loans for basic living costs in western countries should be a source of shame to all their resident Christians, that we have neither given generously from our own riches nor called out our leaders to end injustice and malpractice. It is particularly abhorrent that our own government ends up lending money to people in deep poverty because it refuses to lift those people out of destitution by ensuring enough jobs for all who can work and a liveable alternative for those who can't.

'You make unjust gain by extortion'

Anyone who has ever watched *Yes, Minister* is unlikely to forget it. We see in this series how knowing a little bit of dirt about someone – a past mistake; a previous bowing to pressure; a foolish decision – is used to pressure MPs into further bad decisions. We say that power corrupts, and it is true. It is not just that those in power tend to live and mix with others in similar positions, and gradually forget what life is like for others. It is also that, over time, mistakes build up and these mistakes can be used against policy makers to bend them to the will of those with money.

Imbalances of power act throughout society. In the UK, the insufficient supply of housing means that landlords can raise rents and refuse to carry out repairs, under the threat of evicting the tenant. The tenant has nowhere else to go so cannot complain. The underfunding of the NHS means that it is starting to ration its services to people who meet certain criteria, such as losing weight or giving up smoking – yet those struggling with obesity and smoking need more medical support, not less, to improve their health. Different factions of society may, from time to time, rise to dominance in the media and by publicly condemning those with opposing views can cause those people's careers to fail.

All of these imbalances of power are unjust and unacceptable to God. It is not acceptable to profit out of someone else's suffering. It is not acceptable to put the interests of the rich before the poor, or the interests of yourself before your neighbour or even your enemy.

God calls his people to a more radical love than that; and he calls all leaders to ensure just and equitable countries.

False leaders

Whilst God judged the whole of the Israelite society for sin, he also had specific messages for the leaders. The leaders of society should be better than the people they lead; it should be possible for us to look to our leaders as wiser, maturer people who can guide us in goodness and Godliness. Leaders are meant to care for people in need, defend the weak against the strong, and ensure that everyone is able to live and participate in society. God even required that each king write out the law for himself, keep it with him, and read it all his life.[340]

Instead, the Israelites were led astray by 'prophets' who spoke lies, made false promises of peace, relayed dreams that were not visions from God, and made false boasts.[341] On the basis of these prophets and an arrogant trust in their position as God's people, the Israelites claimed that God would do nothing and that they need not listen to true prophets like Jeremiah.[342] They refused to hear and they considered God's word offensive.[343] They were led astray by false leaders who claimed to have God's word, but who in reality failed to challenge the sin of the Israelites and promised peace when God was sending judgment.

God had called the priests to stand in awe of God, walk in peace and uprightness, and speak only true instruction.[344] But the priests had not fully set their hearts to honour God's name,[345] and had ended up teaching lies and misrepresentations of God's word and commands. The priests broke and disregarded the law and profaned God's sanctuary.[346] Their false teaching had caused many

Israelites to stumble.[347] God therefore judged the priests and caused them to be despised and humiliated.[348] Like the false prophets, they were failing to proclaim to God's people the truth of God's word. They were not ensuring that God's people knew how to live in accordance with God's ways.

The capitals of Israel (Samaria) and Judah (Jerusalem) should have been the places where God was most honoured, yet they had become 'high places' – hilltop locations that were devoted to the worship of false gods.[349] Jerusalem had become a 'city of oppressors, rebellious and defiled'.[350] Her leaders were like 'roaring lions' and 'evening wolves' who left nothing behind in their ravaging of the land.[351] Between them, the very people who were supposed to honour God's name and protect the law instead oppressed the poor, accumulated wealth to themselves, and looked to their own ability rather than to God.[352]

Not only that, but the Israelite leaders could be bought off by the rich – the very rich who, by God's definition, were only rich through theft.[353] They used lies and tricks to trap the innocent and distort justice.[354] They had become 'rich and powerful' and grown 'fat and sleek' by 'catching men' through deceit and by failing to plead the cause of the orphan and defend the rights of the poor.[355] God said that the evil deeds of these people had no limit, and that he should avenge himself for it.[356]

Shepherds and Sheep

In Ezekiel 34, God delivers a scathing indictment of the leaders of Israel. Referring to the people of the land as sheep, God condemns the leaders for not doing their duty by taking care of the flock. Leaders are supposed to be like

191

shepherds taking care of sheep. Leaders are supposed to take action to strengthen those who are weak, bring healing to those who are sick or injured, and find and return those who are lost. Leaders should drive off those who seek to harm their people, and judge between their people when one seeks to harm or oppress another. Leaders should keep their people safe and secure in their home.

Instead of putting their effort into caring for and enabling their people, the leaders had used their people as a source of profit for themselves. They had been harsh and brutal, just like Pharaoh when he enslaved the Israelites and worked them ruthlessly; the same word, *bepharekh*, is used here as in Exodus 1:13-14. It is also the same word used in Leviticus 25:43 when God explicitly forbids ruling ruthlessly – like Pharaoh – over one's employees or indebted peoples. God forbids leaders from acting exploitatively and treating those under them as a source of wealth rather than as people to be protected and provided for. But this was not how the Israelite leaders behaved, and it made God furious.

God rebuked Israel's leaders, saying 'Should not shepherds take care of the flock?'[357] Israel's leaders had not done what leaders should do. Rather than defend the poor and needy against the rich, they judged for a bribe, taught for a price,[358] demanded gifts, and worked together for their own interests.[359] They used deceitful practices and words to harm the poor and benefit themselves;[360] they despised justice and distorted all that was right.[361] 'Even the best of them' was 'like a brier' and 'worse than a thorn hedge'.[362] Yet in all this they did not realise how their behaviour offended God, believing instead that God was among them and would protect them.[363]

God's response was to treat the rich and the leaders

in Israel in the same way that they had treated the poor. They devised many ways for taking poor people's land, livelihoods, and housing away from them. They found ways to give these plans the appearance of legality, following the letter but not the spirit of the law, or changing or creating law to suit their purposes. They took away the basic rights of the least powerful people. So God did the same to them.

Just as richer people had exploited and stolen from the poor, so God took away the exploiters' possessions. [364] God took the land away from the Israelites and gave the northern kingdom to the Assyrians, who repopulated it with people from other conquered nations. The southern kingdom of Judah was given to Babylon. The people's inheritance was gone, leaving them with nothing, with no right of return for the northern Israelites and no return for 70 years for the southern Judeans.

Just as the leaders and the rich did not listen to the needs of the poor, so God did not listen to them.[365] Where previously the poor had laboured and not enjoyed the fruit of their labour, now it was to be the rich who worked but did not get to enjoy the results.[366]

God holds the leaders of a country accountable for how they lead, and a major part of this is how the leaders ensure care and provision for the weak against the strong, the poor against the rich, the sick against the healthy. Leaders are to act like good shepherds, tending for all of their flock, ensuring that everyone's needs are met, and not letting the stronger members harm the weaker. Indeed, action may need to be taken to physically prevent the stronger members of society from bullying, oppressing, or stealing from the poor. This role of justice, order, protection, and provision is a call that God places on all leaders, and Christians have a role in supporting leaders to lead correctly and rebuking them when they don't.

THE ROLE OF GOVERNMENT

In the past in now-developed countries, and in the present in the Majority World, Christians – often as churches, but also as charities or other organisations – have directly organised and paid for key services such as healthcare, education, housing, and the provision of necessities. The recognition that these things are social goods which not everyone can afford – indeed, the majority could not afford – but which everyone should receive led Christians to see themselves as having a duty under God to provide these services out of their own wealth, time, energy, skills, knowledge, and resources.

Some governments and leaders of countries have more opportunities to serve their people than do others. Western countries have high levels of democracy, trust in government, and wealth and resources for governments to legitimately, transparently, and fairly access and utilise. This gives them great opportunity to do great good, far beyond the reach of Christian charity. In other countries, the government lacks legitimacy or honesty to engage in widespread social goods. In these countries, Christian activity may make up a higher proportion of provision of social goods.

Charity, however, has never met the need of poverty. Christians in the 1800s discovered this as they sought to address many societal evils, such as lack of education, poverty, homelessness, and more.[367] In regards to education, by the 1860s 'even the most ardent supporters of 'voluntaryism' had to admit defeat, and the rise of state-organized education dates from the Elementary Education Act of 1870.'[368] Wealthy business owners built housing for the people working in their factories, but reports from the period show that the houses were often cold, damp, and overcrowded. Ian Shaw's book, Evangelicals and Social Action, records even more areas in which voluntaryism had to finally admit that, without government legislation and action, their goals were unachievable.

It is unfeasible to expect Christians today to fulfil on their own the responsibility for preventing and relieving poverty, with no call on governments or rulers to utilise the full resources of a country for the benefit of all citizens and refugees living within it. Generosity is not an answer to injustice. Generosity is the safety net that catches people who slip through justice; it is an add-on, not alternative, to justice. God makes it clear that just as it is not only his own individual people whom he commands to live just and righteous lives, so it is not only his country that he expects to be ruled justly and righteously. God expects of pagan countries and their leaders that they do not oppress their peoples. God expects good government, and is less concerned with how a government obtained power and more with what is done with that power.[369]

Nor does the action of Christians relieve leaders of their responsibility towards the people they rule. God's laws are universal principles for all people, not just for Ancient Israelites in a theocratic nation or Christians as individuals. We know this from the strength of his anger against pagan nations when they did not treat people well. We know it from how angry God is when one person sins against another person. We know it from his command to his people to 'not lose heart in doing good' but to 'do good to all people' 'as we have opportunity'.[370] People in government have the power to affect the life of every person living within their country's borders; because they have the power, they also have the responsibility.

Christian thought over the centuries has recognised and accepted that government is a good. Whilst governments are made up of sinful people, they are also made up of people made in God's image and with the potential for redemption. They are therefore not wholly bad; but at the same time neither are they solely good. Overall, the good and the harm of a government balanced against the good and harm of anarchy is generally considered to come down in favour of government.[371] Had the Israelites never had a leader to bring them together, champion their cause, and direct them as to what to do they would never have left Egypt. Had that leader not delegated justice to seventy wise people, many disputes and issues would never have been settled. Having reached the promised land, the Israelites were unable without a godly leader to remain faithful to God and just in their dealings with one another. The phrase 'each did what was right in his own eyes' is a condemnation of Israel's behaviour at this time. They did not always do much better under their kings, either; a ruler needs to be godly and to have good people to hold him or her to account. But the failures of the kings does not mean that we should settle in favour of anarchy.

There remains, even in a society of sinless persons, the need for organisation, administration, and direction of co-ordinated effort. Without such management, we remain subsistence farmers, never reaching the heights achievable by division of labour. And because there is sin, there is the need also to take action to restrain sin; to have an agreement, as a society, as to which sins merit what form or severity of punishment, and for that punishment to be administered fairly. According to God, the sin that needs to be restrained includes the selfishness that leads to wealth acquisition and inequality to the harm of those with less.

Government is God's servant ordained for our good,[372] even if it fails. Government is there to punish those who do wrong and to commend those who do right.[373] These verses have been interpreted over the centuries to mean that the government has a role in commonwealth – the good of the people rather than the ruler. This common good 'insists that society is more than a series of disconnected, isolated individuals... that every member of society should have a stake in it and be able to exercise meaningful choices within it, and have access to the resources, education, housing, work and relational support which he or she needs to pursue a flourishing human life in all its dimensions.'[374]

Different people have different views on the extent of the role of government, dependent often upon whether they think that government action promotes or harms individual freedom. Stereotypically, economically right-wing views are more common amongst richer people who are more concerned with whether government limits their freedom to acquire and retain wealth. Meanwhile, poorer people are more likely to hold economically left-wing views. In this view, the government plays a key role in ensuring that people at the bottom of society are not left without sufficient means to have freedom in their life to choose such basic things as what food they want to eat, what temperature they'd like to keep their house at, and living standards that are commensurate with good health

– let alone the freedom to 'self-actualise', to direct their life, and to choose the work and other activities that give meaning to their life.

Richard Lowe has articulated four different approaches to the role of government in the common good: the New Right; reluctant collectivism; the Third Way; and democratic socialism.[375] The first three of these are based on capitalism and right-wing economics; only the last takes a left-wing understanding of economics. There may therefore be scope for more approaches to be explored on the left, not least because Lowe's 'democratic socialism' is conflated with social autocracy. Alternatively, one may modify 'the Third Way' to be more concerned with the common good and human welfare, and less reliant on the assumption that capitalism is by default a social good.[376]

The New Right continues with the belief that the unregulated market is the best long-term guarantor of economic efficiency, social justice, and political stability and freedom. Whilst it is recognised that poverty constrains freedom, it is believed that the unregulated market will end poverty. The government's role is restricted to preventing monopolies, cartels, and other ways in which markets cease to be free.

Reluctant collectivists would also like to minimise the role of government in order to maximise individual and political freedom, but they consider that the market does not work without a higher degree of regulation than the New Right would consider acceptable; and they believe that the market on its own can be responsible for 'an unacceptable level of economic waste and social distress.'[377] Reluctant collectivists accept that government intervention can be essential to ensure the positive freedom from poverty and deprivation, whereas the New Right believe that the market will achieve this without government action.

In the Third Way, proponents believe that 'there is no alternative' to capitalism, and that governments should seek to provide the environment in which markets can thrive. In particular, this means an educated, healthy, and mobile workforce; and strong community institutions that maintain the stability and trust that markets need. The government would have a role also in helping the market to shift to new technologies, by educating adults who needed to retrain from an obsolete industry and by protecting people from poverty during such technological shifts. There may be some scope to shift leftwards within the Third Way: a government might consider that there are a number of areas in which markets fail and are better under government provision (e.g. police; justice; healthcare; education), and seek to foster – but also constrain – capitalism only in certain markets that are indeed able to function well, within those appropriate constraints.

Democratic socialists consider that the role of the state is not just to correct market failings, but also to engineer a more equal and fair society. They consider the unregulated market to be not just economically inefficient but also undemocratic, unjust, and unethical. For democratic socialists, the welfare state fosters community and the sense of community within a country. It is the strong foundation on which a thriving economy and society can be built.

What all four of these views on the role of government want is a freedom from poverty for those at the bottom; the opportunity for all to succeed in what they want at life and the freedom to enjoy that success; and a politically and economically successful society over time and place.

But they have very different beliefs regarding how that is obtained. Fortunately, the collection and analysis of data has only increased over the years. We can now consider how different forms of government have performed across the last century and between different countries.

The answer, as it turns out, is relatively simple – at least on the extremes. Contrary to the belief of the New Right, free markets – uncontrolled except for the intervention of governments to prevent monopolies and cartels – do not end poverty and are not economically efficient. Instead, deregulation and small states reduce economic growth compared to economies with higher regulation and more state spending.[378] At the other extreme, a government that 'sought through economic planning to impose a common morality on society would run the risk of becoming, like their predecessors in the German Weimar Republic, "the cultivated parents of a barbarous offspring".'[379] State control of the market is needed, as the reluctant collectivists and Third Way proponents recognise, in order to prevent certain harms and ensure the provision of certain necessities, without which no-one is free. But having ensured those freedoms and prevented those harms, a state that goes too far might start to restrict other freedoms which are also good and important for humanity, such as freedom of conscience and family.

Nevertheless, the evidence indicates that there is room to move further left economically than even our most successful countries, the Scandinavian countries. Although every country has its own unique collection of policies across a huge number of policy areas, the pattern on a wide range of measures is consistent. The more equal countries – the countries which broadly reject the neoliberal/New Right approach, and even go beyond Third Way – perform best.[380] This means that at the very least, higher levels of state action are compatible with – if not direct causes of – greater community cohesion and community spirit. The evidence indicates that none of our modern countries have reached the limit of left-wing economics beyond which the size of the state becomes a problem; instead, there is room to move still further left – for example, by becoming an even larger Welfare State – in order to achieve better results on a wide range of measures, including health, wellbeing, and the economy.

The Welfare State 'is a collection of institutionalized policies and entitlements as social rights, which in various ways offer protection for all who might experience economic and social hardship. The welfare state is, therefore, foremost about the pooling and redistribution of social risks, particularly the risk of income loss.'[381] A key role of the welfare state is to insure people against social risks (in particular illness, disability, and job loss) and to redistribute resources over the life course (e.g., to pay for education for children, collect taxes from working adults, and provide a pension to older adults).[382] The State also covers those costs which are difficult to assign to specific individuals.

Van Kersbergen writes that, 'the welfare state is European in character, because the wide-ranging, interconnected social policies that make up the welfare state reflect the historical European experience of social misery, turmoil, protest, political conflict and war, on the one hand, and reconciliation, cooperation, stability, order, harmony and peace, on the other. The welfare state came to embody a unique answer to the question of how to build and maintain a relatively cohesive economic, social, political and cultural order. Bismarckian social insurances, after all, were not merely pioneered to deal with the social risks of industrial society and to improve workers' living conditions, but they were principally launched to serve the political goals of state- and nation-building and social order. The very term 'welfare state' was popularized, if not invented, by the Archbishop of York, William Temple, who used it in 1941 to contrast this ideal state with the Nazi 'warfare state'.[383]

Some welfare states do better than others. The liberal welfare states (Australia, USA, UK) are very bad at countering the inequality created by private markets. Indeed, they often do not even try to do so: the neoliberal economics on which they are based valorises inequality as a driver of productivity and hard work. In contrast, the generosity of the Nordic states is matched by their high labour market participation; the fear of the right that a strong Welfare State is damaging is not seen in the data. For example, 'welfare state generosity is so far from creating work disincentives that it even increases employment commitment.'[384]

The risk for less-generous Welfare States is that they end up spending just as much, if not more, money on rectifying the problems created by being ungenerous. To a casual observer, this then creates the illusion of a generous Welfare State. But it is not generous to commit to paying for chemotherapy for a Stage 3 cancer patient just because one failed to detect, or act on, a Stage 1 cancer that could have been rectified by a small surgery. The appearance of generosity masks the severe damage caused by allowing a cancer to grow and then having to use highly harmful drugs to treat it later.

An alternative approach to the welfare state is to achieve high levels of equality *before* tax and benefits, like

Japan – but this state of affairs would require very strong political action if it were to be achieved in the UK. It would necessarily mean a dramatic curtailment of income and wealth at the top, perhaps through very high tax rates on excessive incomes. Politically, it is probably more practicable for the UK to take the route of the welfare state than to attempt to achieve Japanese culture and low earnings ratios without Japanese history and Japanese policies on a much wider range of issues. However, the ultimate point remains that a more equal society is better for everyone, whatever the mechanism taken to get there. Neoliberal economics, which sees inequality as a social good, is not one of the mechanisms that achieves a more equal society.

Perhaps other countries, such as African, Asian or Latin American countries, will develop wholly different approaches to government and care for citizens. But in the UK, we are starting from a position of a partially-formed welfare state, which has seen improvements but also retractions over time. We are placed amongst other European and Anglophone countries that also have welfare states, and we can compare the performance of these countries. Amongst these countries, the European Welfare State 'represents a huge accomplishment; thriving economies, liveable and trustful societies and efficient polities are almost unthinkable without it'.[385] Considering all this and the evidence of the benefits of a more equal society, it seems reasonable to conclude that the easiest way for the UK to fulfil the principles of the Old Testament law is for it to invest again in the Welfare State.

CONCLUSION

God calls all people to obedience to him: leaders and lay people; oppressors and oppressed; religious or non-religious. Whoever we are and whatever our role in society, sin is not acceptable to God. Questions of justice and of ensuring the welfare of the poor, needy, and vulnerable are particularly important to God. When we fail on these issues, we dishonour God and may blaspheme his name by misrepresenting him to other people. Leaders have a role in ensuring justice and wellbeing for all their people; and Christians may need to act like biblical prophets in challenging government to act up to its responsibilities. In order to do this, we need to consider carefully what justice and wellbeing looks like both in terms of what the Bible has to say, and in terms of the evidence of what works in developed countries today. We then need to commit to working together to build a society that meets God's standards of what is just and right.

CHAPTER 8

GOD'S ECONOMY: DEBT AND WORK LAWS

GOD GAVE THE ISRAELITES laws on how to manage issues like debt, poverty and unemployment. Although countries today are managed in different ways from Israel's theocratic agrarian society, God's people are still called to follow God's principles for debt and generosity. Steve Orsillo experienced this himself during the 2007/2008 financial crisis. His wife Vicky explains,

'When people owe you money, you notice where they're spending money... [Steve] had gone home and was editing a chapter on the importance of forgiveness... so he felt very convicted to go to every person that rented [one of] our houses and forgive them the debt of their past rent [total $60,000]... we were losing our house, the house was in foreclosure, and we could not get a loan [of $297,000]... that was really hard, but that was when we learned that everything was on the table... Steve called me, and he was very broken, and we just prayed, "Lord, is there anybody who could help us?" A face came to Steve's mind, so Steve called him, and he was very happy to help but whilst he had more than Steve had forgiven in debt, he had less than a third of what Steve needed. So Steve called the bank and said, a man is loaning him $83,000, and he really shouldn't because I'm a really high risk. The bank said, can you do $125,000? But Steve couldn't do that. Steve got an estimate of closing on the house, got back in touch with the bank, and the bank accepted the $83,000 for the $297,000 and forgave the rest.'

Steve says, 'We didn't forgive expecting anything. We forgave because in editing that chapter, I kept reading, "If you forgive, you will be forgiven; and if you don't forgive, you will not be forgiven." And I wasn't thinking in money terms; I wasn't thinking of being forgiven money. I was thinking I need to be forgiven to stand before God. I need to be forgiven, and the way I'm feeling towards these people, I'm probably going to be like that wicked manager, and my debt's going to come back to me. I've been forgiven a lot in my life, and I can't have that be put back on me like it was him. So I said I need to be forgiven, and the Lord laid it on me to go door to door and forgive these people, and I did.'[386]

GOD'S ECONOMY

Israel was an agricultural society. An Israelite's land was used to grow the crops and raise the animals which they ate, converted to clothing, or sold in order to purchase other necessities. Land was an essential private possession which God gave to each person and family according to their need, in order that each had the means to live.[387] Land was not to be accumulated in the way that Ahab thought he could do in buying Naboth's vineyard.[388] Instead, land was the right of you and your descendants to a house and the means of work; it was not a luxury to be traded in accordance with personal desire or individual fortune.

Private property rights were created not to allow the rich to accrue wealth and claim entitlement to keep all of their earnings, but to protect the poor from that very accrual of wealth to the rich. Private property rights meant that the rich *couldn't* buy your home off you, but only (in effect) rent it for a period of less than 50 years. Private property rights meant that the rich *couldn't* accrue property portfolios, because property belonged to the family to whom God first gave it and could never be taken permanently from them. Private property rights acted to protect the poor from the greedy, not to protect the rich from God's demand to give to, provide for, and defend the poor. Indeed, private property rights acted to declare that a range of properties – from land and housing to the crops in your field – actually belonged to whoever needed it.

To lose your land in Israel was to lose not just your home but also the means to support yourself and your family. It was to lose your dignity, independence, and heritage. In today's world, it is like losing your job with no reference at the same time as losing your house with a zero-credit rating. You are forced to be dependent upon the goodwill of others because you have lost the means and dignity of being able to provide for yourself.

But in God's economy, powerlessness never means poverty, because it becomes the responsibility of those with power – with money and means – to care for those without. This could be through one of three means: giving to those in need; redeeming a relative; and hiring (by buying their service for a fixed term of up to six years) a person to work for you.

Giving and lending

If anyone was poor then those with money were commanded to be liberal in helping them.[389] This occurred partly through charity when God commanded his people to give to those in need. But it also occurred through 'enforced' charity, or justice: the centralised collection and redistribution of money in order to give it to those in need.

God contrasts the hard-hearted and tight-fisted, who wickedly refuse to lend to those less likely to repay, with the open-handed who lends freely.[390] Jonathan Burnside points out the contrast between the hard-hearted Pharaoh from whose hand God rescued the Israelites, with the open-hearted, open-handed God.[391] Pharaoh enslaved the Israelites, made them provide their own straw for the bricks that they were required to make for the Egyptians, and refused to give the Israelites any time off to worship God. God rescued the Israelites, provided them with land to meet their needs, and gave them a system of Sabbaths for rest. God's command is therefore not merely economic but also social and political: who will you be like, God or Pharaoh?

Repayment of debt was not necessary in God's economy. Although a helped person was presumably to repay if they became able to do so, this is not specifically mentioned, and every seventh year was a year of debt relief. Being close to that seventh year, and therefore unlikely to get any loan repaid, was not an acceptable reason to limit generosity. Indeed, to even think in such a way was wicked and sinful. The least credit-worthy (those least likely to repay, because the seventh year was near) were to be lent to as freely as those who would almost certainly repay; and no loan could persist more than seven years.

In practice this meant that loans to the least credit-worthy or 'undeserving' were gifts, not loans – making God's economy one in which the undeserving can end up receiving even more than do the deserving. Such radical grace is at the heart of Christianity: Jesus notes that it is those who have been forgiven much who love much;[392] in a parable of vineyard workers, those who worked the least got the same pay – and therefore higher hourly pay – as those who worked the most;[393] and the thief dying on the cross with no opportunity for future obedience to God was as forgiven as Zacchaeus, who repaid fourfold anyone he had cheated and gave away half of what he had left over. Jesus confirms this model for Christians: we are to lend without expecting repayment, for if we lend only to those who can repay then we are no better than sinners. Indeed, not only are we to lend without repayment, but we are to lend without repayment to our enemies.[394]

To further ensure that those who would struggle to repay could not be chased for payment or left worse off than before, God prohibited lenders from taking, as a pledge or repayment, anything that a person needed for life, dignity, and work such as their cloak (to be returned each sunset, to keep the debtor warm)[395] and millstone (means of work, for grinding grain).[396] A lender could not go into a person's home to take a pledged item as security, thus invading privacy and exacting control, but must let the person bring it out.[397] God's focus here is the protection of the poor person, not of the rich; if the poor person cannot repay, it is the rich person who loses out.

God also forbade the collection of interest.[398] Having already ensured that all debts were cancelled every seventh year, forbidden the proximity of this year as an excuse not to lend, and restricted what could be taken as pledge, God then made it even harder for lending to be a commercial transaction by forbidding interest. Lending was emphatically not about making money but about helping those in need. It was not about the financial interests of the lender but about the need of the recipient. For the lender, it is about making the choice: will you act like God, or like Pharaoh? It is not just a matter of economics, but of the entire shape and orientation of society. It is not just a question of private morals, but of the legal system and how to govern a country – for the good of the poor, or for the good of the rich.

Furthermore, the Israelites were not to harvest their crops so thoroughly as to leave nothing behind, but rather were to deliberately leave fruit on the vine and grain in the field for poor Israelites and foreigners to collect for themselves.[399] Any person walking through a crop could also take food to eat as they passed; not sitting down to eat, nor collecting to take away, but merely meeting an immediate need in passing.[400] Thus even the poorest, most indebted Israelite always had a means to provide for themselves through the gleanings of another's field, the protection of clothing, and the retention of necessary tools such as millstones. In this way, God validates both personal effort (the poor have to go out to glean, although they did not have to be involved in the work of ploughing, sowing, weeding, and other agricultural chores) and structural justice (it is a legal requirement that there is a form of work that the poor can do to access food or money; and that those with money or resources make it available to the poor). God also overturns the claim of the land or business owner to keep all the fruit or profit of his labour, by requiring that a portion of it be given to the poor and hungry. Meeks says of this that 'gleaning rights are not voluntary acts of charity of the rich toward the poor; they are the poor's right to livelihood.'[401] This is a legal requirement of justice, not an optional action of charity.

Redemption and recovery

If an Israelite did end up in the situation of selling their home and land, then this too was never a permanent situation. Whenever possible, a relative was to come and buy back the land from the purchaser.[402] This meant that the land remained within a given family, clan, or tribe. If a relative could not or did not buy the land, then at that point it could be sold to someone else. But come the Jubilee year, that land would go back to its original owner, regardless of who had bought it.

All Israelites therefore had a duty towards an impoverished person, to help them in their need. In this instance, the purchase of someone's land released money for the impoverished person. But the return of the property in the Jubilee year meant that no person, let alone their descendants in perpetuity, could be left without the means to be restored in society.

In the UK, the absence of such a procedure as Jubilee has had major consequences. In centuries past, the average member of the public had rights of common use over large areas of land in the area that they lived. They had the right to graze animals on this land and to collect what they needed in terms of food and fuel from the land. Enclosure Acts allowed rich landowners to 'buy' the right to common land from the poor. But the money paid could in no way compensate for future generations' loss of the right to grazing and foraging.[403] Instead, it meant a consolidation of wealth with the already-wealthy, and the displacement of the rural poor in perpetuity. A Jubilee Act would have prevented this.

The corollary of Jubilee is that wealth could never be accumulated permanently – if indeed anyone could still be wealthy after the generous giving and lending without repayment that was commanded. There was a divinely-installed reset and redistribution that maintained and restored the equality and dignity of every individual. No poor person could sell in perpetuity the ability of their descendants to meet their needs; no rich person could acquire for their descendants the ownership of that which God said belonged to the descendants of the poor person.

This reset, however, applied only to what was needed for decent lifestyles and access to home and work. It applied to the rural land, which was the foundation of the economy and society, but property in a city only had the right of redemption for up to a year.[404] City-based properties at that time were superfluous, luxury items which God did not protect. If someone who had previously bought a city property then later had to sell it, they did not get it back at the Jubilee. As long as they had what they needed – the agrarian home and land – then they did not need to be restored to luxury. God wanted the necessities and some elegancies of life to be protected, but he did not protect the luxuries. Some difference in luxuries was acceptable so long as everyone first had a decent living standard.

Work and Pay

In some cases, Israelites would have to hire themselves out to other Israelites or even foreigners if they were to earn money to buy bread. In these instances, God made provisions to ensure that those in powerless positions were not taken advantage of by those who, by virtue of land ownership, had control over the jobs market. Those who retained their land – whether through good fortune, inheritance, or hard work – were to take responsibility for those who lost theirs – regardless of whether it was lost through misfortune or lack of effort.

God expected good conditions and decent pay for his people who were in paid employment. Workers should be able 'to live among you' and not suffer from poverty, live in degrading or segregated circumstances, or have to leave for another land in search of food and income.[405] Payment for work should be made promptly and reliably – daily, in Israelite society – to ensure that a person was able to meet his needs as they occurred.[406]

'Living among you' would have meant that there was no geographical distinction between poorer and richer areas, as there are in the UK today; people of all wealths would have lived amongst one another in a mixed society. The cycle of deprivation that can afflict an area as people who attain higher incomes move out, and people on lower incomes or less able to work move in, should not have happened. It is not 'living among you' when richer people live in different, more pleasant and more invested-in parts of the country than poorer people. 'Living among you' would also have meant an income and status that was adequate for full social participation, not just enough to get by or a stigma attached to those in poverty.

There was to be no exploitation of hired labour. Workers were not to be treated harshly or ruled over without compassion, and in particular Israelites were to look out for those in the employ of foreigners to ensure that there was no exploitation or harsh treatment. Little tricks, such as charging a profit for food supplied to one's workers, were also outlawed.[407] And at the end of six years, servants were not merely to be set free but showered liberally with gifts, beyond the value of their work.[408] The generosity shown was to be commensurate not with the value of the labourer or their alleged 'worthiness', but with the riches given by God to the employer.

Again there is the contrast with Pharaoh: the same rare word, *bepharekh*, is used in Leviticus 25 as Exodus 1:13-14 to refer to ruthless rule. Pharaoh's trick of making the Israelites supply their own straw for bricks is not to be repeated by the Israelites, and nor is Pharaoh's refusal to let the people go. Pharaoh wanted to extract all the worth he could from the Israelites; God utterly forbids such behaviour and even commands the opposite – giving generously to the worker. In terms of how we treat our employees, we should strive to be the opposite of Pharaoh and to be as godly as God.

Workers should never be paid less than they are worth, for God forbids gaining any increase (profit) from them; the implication is that all value created by the worker is paid to the worker (if the worker does so little that his or her work does not earn a liveable income, then the laws of gleaning and generosity would come into play). This is in addition to bans on usury and requirements to write off debt in the seventh year. God therefore forbids the better-off and more powerful from profiting from either another person's labour (by underpaying them) or their misfortune (by lending at interest, failing to write-off debt, or over-charging them for necessities like food).

The type of mass redundancies seen when an entire business closes or industry fails, such as in the UK government's closure of coal mines, was not possible under Israel law because of the duty of the employer to secure the wellbeing of the employee. Far from being a question of slavery and the rights of the master over the slave, Israelite employment was a question of the duties of the employer to look after, protect, and ensure the full well-being of the employee.

Why care?

God gives us three reasons why we should be concerned about the pay and working conditions of people in poverty. We should be concerned firstly because we know what it feels like; secondly, as a response of gratitude to God; and thirdly, because we reflect God's character.

Firstly, because we know what it feels like. In Deuteronomy, God reminds his people that they were slaves in Egypt. God uses this reasoning several times when he is explaining his laws to his people. The fact that the Israelites had been slaves in Egypt should have meant that they had compassion on people in similar circumstances; a shared experience which made them feel sorrow for anyone else in poverty and which stirred them to action. This was the case even though the slavery in Egypt was a historical event that later Israelites had not experienced.

We haven't been slaves in Egypt either, and many western Christians don't know what it's like to be poor and to have your choices, and in particular your desire to better yourself or just to participate in your local community, be constrained by a lack of money. But we do know what it is like to be a slave to sin, to addictions, and to self-seeking behaviour. A slave cannot do what he or she pleases, but most obey the master. We are all slaves either to sin or to Jesus; if to sin, then we are unable to resist sin; if to Jesus, then we must obey Jesus. Even now as Christians and slaves to Jesus, we still find ourselves sinning. So we know what it is like to be constrained to do what we do not want to do, even in adequate material circumstances. We know, or should know, that it is not a situation we should want to see other people in, especially when heightened by poverty and material lack. The way we act shows whether or not we identify with those who are suffering and the extent of our own awareness of our previous slavery to sin and ongoing failure to obey God.

Secondly, we should care about poor people out of gratitude to God. Just as God brought the Israelites out of Egypt, he has through Christ's death redeemed us from sin. When we understand what that means, it naturally evokes a response in us of gratitude to God. We should want to return God's generosity to him; and the way that he has provided for us to do that is through our actions towards others. Unlike the servant who, having been forgiven his debt, went out and imprisoned a man in debt to him, we should extend the forgiveness we have received from God to other people. God himself expects our faith in him to result in generosity to the poor, and questions the validity of our claimed faith if it does not. The generosity of Christ to us should result in our generosity to others. The kindness that God shows in not demanding from us what we are not capable of, and his care in providing for us all that we need, should be shown in turn to the people we encounter. The way we act shows how well we have understood what God does for us.

Finally, we should care about poor people because we reflect God's character. God cares about poor people: the Bible is full of verses where God declares his concern for the poor and commands us to join him in defending them. The way we act shows people what God is like. We are mirrors of his glory and grace – or we should be. Too often we show only the same sinfulness and greed as the rest of society. Instead we should act out God's love and generosity to the poor people of our nations. In this way,

216

we honour and bring glory to God; when we don't, we dishonour and blaspheme him, and the rest of our worship becomes a stench to him.

LEADERS

Leaders have an even greater responsibility than do individual citizens. They are the ones who govern the systems in which people live and work. They can permit or encourage bad working practices, inequality, and systematic injustice. They can also protect people from exploitation.

In the book of Micah, God challenges both the religious and the political leaders. He condemns the religious leaders who have insisted that God is not angry with his people and that he will not do harm to them, even though the Israelites are oppressing the poor. He condemns the political leaders who 'despise justice and distort all that is right', accepting bribes and working for their own benefit instead of that of the poor.[409] God is angry because he cares about the poor, and yet his leaders have not only failed to protect the poor but have actively harmed them and encouraged the people to think that God is not angry because of this. God is not pleased with us when we ignore the plight of those in need and selfishly seek only the best bargains for ourselves.

The religious leaders supported and encouraged the political leaders, saying whatever the political leaders wanted to hear. They insisted that Israel and the Israelites could do no wrong. They repeatedly neglected God's laws of economic and social justice whilst claiming that obedience to the sacrificial and cleanliness laws meant that the Israelites were right before God. Thus they not only permitted sin amongst their people but actively told them that this was okay. In contrast, our religious leaders should be calling out sin both amongst God's people and amongst the leaders of the country.

JUSTICE AND GENEROSITY

In Israel, every person in the nation was responsible as a servant of God for ensuring that everyone had what they needed to survive. The result of God's laws for Israel was that all Israelites were responsible for ensuring that fellow Israelites in poverty had access to money, food, a place to live, and a place to work. This could be by lending (not at interest), giving, distributing tithes, redeeming, or employing. The same laws did not apply to foreigners, to whom Israelites could lend at interest, and who were not released from debt or slavery on a periodic basis. However, Israelites were still supposed to help foreigners who were in need.

Importantly, this was to be provided not only or even chiefly through charity, but through the dignity of the economic structure of society. What God has to say to the Israelites about poverty therefore has a bearing not just on our private lives and use of money, but on our political and public lives and any roles we have as decision makers in business or politics. It has a bearing on how countries should be run and what leaders should be aiming to provide or ensure.

God's laws created in effect a welfare state that was partly central (the collection and distribution of tithes every third year); partly legal and redistributive (interest on lending was banned; employees had to be treated well and released on a periodic basis; parts of the harvest belonged as of right to those in need; a person's access to home, self-employment, and subsistence living was redistributed every 50 years); and partly private and social (redeeming relatives; giving to the needy). That is, the prevention and alleviation of poverty came about through direct government action; through laws regulating public, private, and business behaviour; and through the action taken by individuals to take responsibility for the needs of others. The outcome of such laws would have been the abolition of poverty and the guarantee for everyone of a secure home and means of work. It would have also meant the prevention of the accumulation of wealth (and power) by a minority, and a substantially more equal society than is in existence today in the UK.

Reflecting on this helps us to consider how we should treat people today. God's nation had a welfare society, but it was smaller than many modern welfare states because God's people carried a high personal responsibility to end poverty and because the main form of provision was through subsistence farming. When a small number of people dwell in a land much larger than their needs, simply having access to a home and land is enough. But in modern society, where governments over the centuries have permitted economic change in a way that means the poor cannot access subsistence farming or foraging rights, there is a need to develop a different way to ensure that everyone has a home, means to live, and participation in society.

Nicholas Townsend argues that whilst 'the Christian polity is the primary mode by which God wishes to bring into being good relations among people', nevertheless 'if there are social preconditions of this happening... establishing them must be the role of political authority in the secular polity.' He gives the example of a book launch, which to be successful requires such things as 'the venue, the chairs, the lighting, the transport network; the conditions of human living of those who attend: food and water, good enough health, freedom to come' as preconditions. But to be successful, it needs more than that: 'people actually need to be there, to speak, to listen.'[410] The role of government, then, is 'to secure the social conditions necessary for the possibility of the common good.' If some people lack access to such preconditions, then 'they are being excluded from the very possibility for the life God intends for them – even though establishing these conditions is not the same thing as directly generating the common good itself.'[411] There are certain organisation and administrative roles that fall to a government even in a perfect society, to achieve the coordination of labour that allows us to rise above subsistence living.

Jobs and income security

God's laws for Israel gave wealthier Israelites the responsibility to employ or otherwise provide for poorer Israelites, through moral laws on generosity and state laws on structural justice and redistribution. The result was a system that guaranteed work or income.

Empirically, the responsibility for full employment in developed countries has to lie with the government, as it is the only body with the size and power to guarantee it. Individuals do not have the scope to employ and guarantee employment to every person in the country. Nor can we encourage people to live as subsistence farmers and expand into business if their farming thrives: there simply isn't enough farmable, accessible land in the UK. And private businesses cannot employ every person in the country who wants and is able to work: we have tried this approach since the 1980s, and have never had full employment since then.

Unemployment harms the economy because of the useful work that is not done, the harmful effects to the unemployed, and the damaging work practices that high unemployment enables. Job insecurity is more common in countries with high unemployment because employers don't have to worry about retention when they can easily replace staff; and job insecurity is bad for employees.[412] Across countries, rates of unemployment are correlated with suicide rates. The size of this effect, however, varies according to how generous – how adequate – that country's unemployment benefits are.[413] That is, a government can mitigate the harm of unemployment experienced by unemployed people by increasing the financial support available to them.

Yet when government policy decisions in the early 1980s caused unemployment to shoot up from one million to three million, the government of the day did not see this as a failure of its policy or as an indicator of its duty to ensure the creation of other jobs for those people whose jobs were destroyed. Instead, the government took the opposite position and decided to blame these people for their lack of a job, calling them skivers and scroungers even though they had been working right up to the point that a change in government and government policy caused a shortage of jobs. The economic and political harm caused by this approach continues today, as the narrative of 'scrounger' has allowed governments over the decades to erode the welfare state and place increasingly punitive requirements on unemployed people to find work. Yet the primary contributor to whether a person finds work or not is the availability of work in their local area – not their education; not their 'work ethic' (which in any case is generally strong and tenacious[414]); not their upbringing.

And it is the government that sets the rules of the economic society which determines the number of jobs available in the country.

Currently the UK government provides destitution-level support to people who have not got work but are looking for it.[415] What if instead the government paid this financial support as a wage for work done in the local community? There is no evidence that the demeaning, demoralising, and de-skilling 'work-search' of the current approach has any beneficial impact for long-term employment rates and earnings.[416] Yet for the same – though ideally more – money, the government could have useful work done. When this is done well, it is called a Job Guarantee and it ensures far more than the financial support of those whom the private sector does not want: it also maintains and increases skills, helps the local community, provides evidence of work ability to private employers, and drives up standards in the private sector without the burden of enforcing legislation.

The private sector cannot employ a person if there isn't enough demand for the product of that additional person's labour. But the government can always employ a person in a community-oriented role because the government benefits from wider societal gains than just a monetary profit (and conversely, suffers from negative societal consequences of unemployment). These may include such things as improved wellbeing of both the worker and the people or community being served; gains in environmental health; up-skilling of workers; and increased community cohesion and trust. By saving people from boredom, frustration, and poverty, the government may also gain from reductions in illness, drug misuse, and criminality. The private sector has a very narrow financial profit on which it bases its decisions; the government has a much wider social and environmental benefit to consider, as well as its moral duty before God. The result is that work which is unprofitable for the private sector is nevertheless highly beneficial and profitable for the government to pay a citizen to do.

Jobs themselves should pay the Living Wage. A living wage reflects the idea that there is a minimum value to an hour of a person's time, based on the inherent value of humans and their need in the modern economy to earn money at a rate that is not exploitative. All jobs should pay at least the rate required for a single person to participate in society, in order to prevent exploitation, exclusion, and poverty. This would progress the labour market towards Biblical principles of not just paying a labourer based on what the employer thinks they're worth, but paying generously and ensuring that all residents of the country can participate in, and are not excluded from, society due to poverty. If a business cannot survive except by exploiting the labour of others, then it does not deserve to survive. Using such arguments to support under-payment and over-work for employees comes under God's ban on wicked schemes and lies dreamt up to oppress the poor.[417]

The overall evidence is that there is no impact of raising the National Minimum Wage (NMW) on UK employment rates.[418] Overall, there is no reduction in employment levels or hours of work after an increase in the NMW, and nor are people more likely to be 'let go' if the minimum wage is increased during a person's term of employment. Having said that, some sub-groups may be slightly negatively affected: part-time employees may be slightly more likely to be let go if there is an increase in the NMW (although not during the 2007-10 recession); and an increase in the NMW of 10% may result in a decrease in part-time employment of 1.2%. But these small and isolated harmful effects could easily be counter-acted by government policy in other areas, such as a Job Guarantee or a higher social security rate for unemployed and low-employed people.

Overall, when negative effects of raising the NMW are present, they tend to be so marginal as to be economically and socially irrelevant, with such small impacts that they are easily swamped by other contributors to employment levels, including contributions which the government can make in order to counter any negative effects. It is plausible that at some point the NMW is so high as to have a negative impact overall, but we do not appear to be anywhere close to that point at the moment, which leaves us with plenty of room to bring the NMW up to the Minimum Income Standard for a single person.

Because some people cannot work – whether because of illness, disability, caring duties, lack of jobs for everyone, or other valid reason – there will still be a need for social security. In the Old Testament, this was seen through the laws on gleaning and tithes, but also in legal restrictions on the right of the rich to profit from the poor, the ban on interest on loans and on profiting from food sold to workers, and the command to forgive loans every seventh year. The Israelite state ensured access to employment for those who could work; access to centralised, effective, and efficacious support for those who couldn't; and additional support commanded through private charity as well as bans on any form of profiteering or exploitation. The Israelite nation functioned as a state to protect and provide for the poor through law and economic structures, as well as commanding individual generosity on top of state support. Neither state support nor private generosity on its own was enough: we need both.

Housing

The second major aspect of the Israelites' welfare system was to ensure access to housing. There was a requirement on extended family to buy a family member's house if a person was in such poverty as to need to sell their home. An impoverished person could also work as a form of indentured servant, with their employer responsible for their welfare until the Jubilee came round and the person's house was restored to them. The system therefore ensured housing through the laws placed on family, employers, and wider society.

In modern states, there is no ancestral right to land as there was for Israel. We can't therefore recreate the system of Jubilee, giving every person in the UK a house and piece of land to farm (would you like an acre of Ben Nevis to live and work on? How about an acre under the Thames?). The principle of security of housing therefore has to be met in a different way. Yet as with jobs, where the private sector simply cannot guarantee to provide a job for everyone, the private sector in the UK cannot and does not provide houses for everyone.

Even when some major mill owners built housing for their workers, this was no more an act of charity than when a housebuilder builds a house to sell or rent out. It was a pragmatic decision to ensure that workers could live nearby. Some millowners did build decent housing in decent living environments, but many workers lived in cramped, cold, and damp conditions that contributed to their general ill-health. In these instances, the mill owner had acted not out of charity, let alone justice, but out of exploitation: making money off the necessity of his workers to have a home and live near work, by offering only an inadequate, over-priced place to rent. You only have to read an Elizabeth Gaskell or Charles Dickens book to see the appalling conditions in which most factory workers lived and worked. This exploitation and profiteering off another's need is condemned by God.

There was more freedom, in a much less populated Britain, to build houses where they were needed without a central government organising where houses should go. Whilst there would still have been local objections and constraints based on who owned and was willing to sell land, nevertheless the supply of land was such that it was usually possible to find somewhere else to buy and build on. For example, Victorian railways did not always follow the optimal route, because a landowner would refuse to sell the required land. But this did not mean that railways could not be built at all, just that they had to take an inferior route according to what land could be bought.

But in modern Britain, where every square foot of land is owned and we don't have enough farmland, wild nature, and access to natural spaces, the location of new houses has to be carefully thought about. The question of whether the local roads can take the extra traffic, the local schools and GPs serve the additional population, and local nature can survive further fragmentation all have to be considered. This requires co-ordination and thought at the national level, to meet both the national need for more housing and ancillary services, and local need to not cause excessive harm to existing residents.

Again it falls on the government to ensure housing. When governments stopped building as many social houses from the 1980s onwards, the private sector did not

– because it could not – fill in the gap. The private sector simply cannot build houses to sell at a loss to those who cannot afford the market price. Consequently, whilst the private sector builds as many houses as ever, there has been a national housing shortage for decades due to the failure of the government to build housing for those who cannot afford the full cost.[419] And whilst there have been and continue to be cases where charities and even businesses build houses, this has never been enough to meet the need.

But the government has the power to buy the most appropriate land on which to build housing; the ability to determine how many houses of what size are needed where and with what additional infrastructure; and the capacity to choose to spend on the building of houses. As with a Job Guarantee, only the government can guarantee that there is enough housing for everyone and that that housing is decent; the government therefore has the responsibility to do this, and is unjust and immoral when it does not.

In contrast to relying on charity, evidence shows that simply providing housing is a good way to end homelessness. Many homeless projects try to progress homeless people through a variety of night-shelters, hostels, rehabilitation centres, and shared accommodation before affording someone the dignity of their own home. These come with multiple problems including high costs and substandard living conditions from over-crowding, unhygienic and unsafe properties, and the natural consequences of mixing people with similar (often drug and mental health related) problems in the same environment and expecting them not to have negative consequences for each other. In Finland, a policy of providing housing first *alongside* the wider support they need has proved highly effective: four in five transition into a stable life; and Finland is the only European country in which homelessness is declining.[420]

The central government has the over-arching ability and duty to ensure that everyone is housed, and it should make use of its ability and meet its duty. To fail to do so is a moral issue. This does not mean that private and charitable constructions are banned, but that they supplement the government provision. They can act as trailblazers for new construction techniques and show how to build the kinds of houses that people want to live in. But they cannot, and will not, ever meet the need in the way that is needed. For a country to not collectively act to ensure housing for all its citizens is for us to fail God's call for justice and the wellbeing of the poor. For Christians not to care about this is to imply that God does not care about people's living conditions either.

Health and social care

Israel did not have a healthcare system laid out in its law. There were public health regulations (around the spread of communicable diseases, which were described as making a person or object unclean; and around other practices, such as sexual behaviours, which would also have helped safeguard health), but there was no centrally funded medical system. Churches, however, have often taken on these roles, and it has been in part the example of churches that has prompted governments to take on the responsibility themselves. The Christian faith teaches that every person – whether in-group or out-group, rich or poor, friend or enemy – has worth and should be treated with charity and dignity. This includes treating those who are sick and providing support to those who are disabled.

It is clear from the Bible that people could experience

devastating healthcare costs, as in the case of the woman who had experienced twelve years of haemorrhage and had spent all she had on physicians. This is surely not what God wants for his people: that they be left to render themselves destitute through healthcare costs, rather than helped by those with means to access healthcare. Unfortunately, charity has never yet proved adequate. It is inefficient, undignified, and leaves many needs unfunded. We cannot rely on rich people using their wealth to fund the needs of poor people, especially when those riches were accrued through unjust behaviours.

The problem with healthcare is that it can be very expensive and it does not fall evenly on society. Some people enjoy good health for decades; others suffer genetic disorders, major injury, or reaction to infectious disease like COVID-19 that leaves them disabled for the rest of their lives. This occurs both to people who have always abided by good health behaviours and continue to do so, and to people on the lower margins of society where healthy eating may be unaffordable, the nature of work is such that it often causes or contributes to long-term ill-health,[421] and the simple stress of being lower down the social hierarchy leads to worse health.[422] Nor can we even refrain from any illness- or injury- inducing activity: just walking down the stairs poses the risk of a deadly fall, but not moving will not do us any good either; and whilst some sports are also high risk for injury, I've never seen calls for people who are injured through sport to fund their own healthcare because it's their 'fault'.

Because the cost of healthcare does not fall evenly, it is both impossible (for the many poor people) and inefficient (for everyone) if every person and family has to have constantly laid by enough money to cover the costs of healthcare in the event of needing it. This is foolish even for the very rich: most of them won't need the cost of expensive healthcare, and so for most of them it is a waste of the money to set it aside indefinitely and ultimately needlessly, rather than to spend it now.

Far more sensible is for each person to contribute a smaller sum towards the potential cost of healthcare. This sum is then stored in a national pot. Some people, by chance, won't end up needing it, but they could not have predicted that in advance so would otherwise have had to store up even more money to cover healthcare just in case they did need it. Paying a smaller sum is better than having to indefinitely set aside a larger sum. This is the principle of insurance: everyone contributes a small amount in order to cover expenses that would exceed many people's resources and for others would mean having to set aside money that could otherwise be spent on useful or enjoyable items. When the insurer is the government or a not-for-profit organisation, rather than a private company with a profit motive, then the effect is one of a community supporting its members in the event of ill-health, injury, or impairment. This is a profoundly Biblical and Christian approach which should be encouraged. It is also pragmatically the only sensible approach for the majority, and the only affordable approach for the poor.

The same principles apply to social care. The cost of social care can rapidly consume and exceed the state pension and is therefore unreachable for the majority of people. And like healthcare, the cost of social care falls unevenly: a cancer patient is treated on the NHS, but a dementia patient may need years of social care; a healthy octogenarian may die with minimal care needs, but others spend decades needing care which easily outstrips their resources.

This is not a kind way to treat people. It goes against all of God's principles and his creation of us in his image. It is not viable for most people, let alone every person, in the country to seek to fund their own health and social care. It means that a sick or disabled person ends up paying twice: once through their illness or disability, and a second time through the loss of money. Meanwhile, charity is not only undignified to the recipient but also subject to the whims of the donors, with money going to those areas that are most popular rather than the most needy. The only efficient and efficacious way to fund health and social care is some sort of pooled resources, providing care that is free-at-the-point-of-use and in relation to which any payment or compulsory insurance (which is no different from a tax) is set according to ability to pay and not according to factors such as disadvantage, lifestyle (whether fitness freak engaged in high-risk sport or couch potato with minimal injury risk) or genetic dispositions – many of which are associated with lower income.

Mixing church and state

The state has an important role to play in society. As well as the pillars of employment, income, housing, healthcare, social care, and education, the state also provides key infrastructure like roads, sewage, and utilities; and maintains security and peace through the police, criminal justice system, and armed forces. These should be provided by government because that is the most effective and efficient way to ensure access to these necessities by everyone. Some people with additional means may choose to spend extra money on, for example, private healthcare, education, security, and legal advice, but the fact that the majority cannot do this means that there is a need for good quality state provision. To not offer this to poor people means that they are made vulnerable to exploitation by the greater resources and power of the rich. This is particularly well seen in criminal justice, where outcomes can be influenced far too heavily by which side has the most money to spend on legal fees.

Allowing richer people to access the same state resources (rather than using means-testing to deny them the same state provision that everyone else gets) seems to me to be a fair recompense for their financial contributions to society – especially when many won't actually use the offered resources anyway! It also helps rich people to become more aware of the provision and benefits that they receive from living in a developed country, and prevents the divisive feeling that poor people get more whilst rich people give more.

However, in some countries there is a particular antipathy to the state and state provision, including or even especially from Christians. There is a worry that government provision means that one is ultimately looking to the government for provision, rather than relying on and looking to God. This leads to policy positions that directly harm the poor by cutting spending on social security, healthcare, social care, education, housing, and jobs. In order for a Christian to hold to this anti-government position, it is necessary for this position to be strongly supported both theologically – God does not expect the government to support its citizens – and empirically – these direct harms create an environment where they are outweighed by the indirect benefits.

There is, however, good theological support for the idea that God does expect the government to care for its citizens. If God did not appoint this role to leaders, then he would not have moved against pagan nations for failing to act justly and to support and defend the poor. If society could function well without a degree of centralised control and provision, then the Israelites would not have fallen into chaos every time a judge died; and God would not have given them laws that included the centralised organisation of society. Our leaders and governments have that authority from God for our good.[423] They should use it for our good, and we should encourage them to do so and call them to account when they don't. This is true regardless of how the government obtained its power: God is less concerned with how governments obtain power, and more concerned with what they do with that power once they have it.[424]

The risk is that what starts as mistrusting the government gradually morphs into the church becoming a mini state-within-a-state.

In many areas, we simply can't or shouldn't withdraw from the state. Do we really want to argue that Christians should withdraw from state criminal justice? Should Christians seek to run their own police, security forces, judges, and penal programmes? What about roads and utilities – should Christians take over the responsibility for building and maintaining roads, in order that we should not become overly dependent upon the government and forget to look to God for this provision? Should we deal with our own waste and run our own recycling and sewage treatment plants? It simply isn't practicable for Christians to withdraw from all state provision. The question is merely which areas should come under state provision.

Furthermore, it is a flawed theology to imply that accessing state support is an act of faithlessness. God may call some people to leave the UK and serve in countries where they will have to pay for healthcare, but that does not mean that countries with the stability and the resources to run a state healthcare system have no responsibility to do so or that Christians should not call for such a system. God may equally call a Christian to move to a country that lacks good roads, waste disposal, and sewage. That doesn't mean that governments shouldn't be expected to maintain key infrastructure, or that Christians in these countries shouldn't get involved in creating a government-funded waste disposal system.

Accessing state support is not an example of trusting in something other than God. It is an act of thankfulness to God that he has provided this particular means of support not only to us but to a great many more people who are in need. It is an act of thankfulness that this particular means of support is not only ostensibly available to us, but actually available to us. It is in recognition that God can provide in many different ways, and we should not refuse one of the options out of a misguided idea that it is more faithful to receive from God in a different way.

More fundamentally, for anyone who does rely on long-term state support, it is in recognition that governments can and do take away structures of support over a mere handful of years. We are acutely aware, having watched governments strip away our support, that the support available to us now may not be available in a few years' time. We might be re-assessed for benefits and be told that our long-term, unchanging (except to get worse) illness or disability has somehow disappeared even as we know it hasn't. We might be on a waiting list that is years long for treatment or therapy. We might have the amount of money we receive cut from one year to the next, or see inflation out-strip benefit rates. State provision is not an alternative to trusting in God; it is a means by which God may provide, but it is insecure like all other forms of provision. The ultimate security is from God.

CONCLUSION

God has certain expectations of a just society to ensure that everyone can lead a decent life. This means that society needs to organise itself in way that meets these expectations. Practically speaking, this has implications for government, and especially for democratically elected governments in developed countries. Christians should seek to hold the government to account on its role and responsibility, and call on all people to work for the sort of fair and just society that God expects.

It is not a failure of trust in God to believe that the government has certain responsibilities towards citizens, nor is it wrong to ask the government to meet these responsibilities. Instead, to declare to society and government that there are certain things which all people should be able to access is a declaration of God's justice and goodness. To hold government to account on this is to say that how our leaders behave and how our society is set up are matters of importance to God. He expects a degree of socio-economic justice which our current levels of inequality and poverty do not permit, and which will not be achieved whilst governments neglect their role in ensuring adequate provision of key goods such as housing, income, and work.

CHAPTER 9
TRUE CHRISTIANITY

THERE SEEMS TO ME to be a general order for what is considered to be most important in obedient Christianity: firstly, attend church and at least feel guilty about not being more interested in Bible study and prayer; secondly, keep sex within a heterosexual monogamous marriage (serial monogamy via divorce may be okay); then maybe engage in some form of evangelism or at least invite work colleagues to a carol concert or other relatively middle-class, 'quality' event; and then last and least of all is what may actually be closer to God's heart than church attendance: social action.

Amongst middle-class Western evangelical Christians there has been a tendency to reject social action as a hangover from Catholic works-based salvation. All that is required is sexual purity and church attendance, with perhaps some attendant guilt about not being evangelistic enough. But this is behaving just like the Pharisees: people who focused on prayer, inward piety, and the study of Scripture but neglected the fact that God's righteousness includes grace and social justice.

What the Pharisees did instead was to lay on people burdens that could not be met. Rather than generously help the undeserving, they prescribed rules about how to behave. Jesus called these rules 'heavy, cumbersome loads' and condemned the rule-givers who did 'not lift a finger to move' these burdens or help the carriers.[425] Jesus, in contrast, offers a light burden and easy yoke.[426] There are no endlessly long rules or rituals or regulations with Jesus. Following Jesus is challenging, but it is the challenge of self-sacrifice and death, not the challenge of constantly keeping more rules than it is possible to remember.

It is said that a Gentile once asked two Rabbis to explain the Torah to him in great brevity (whilst 'standing on one foot'). One, Shammai, sent him away on the grounds that this was not possible, but Hillel replied, 'What is hateful to you, do not do to your fellow. That is the whole Torah; the rest is the explanation – now go and study.' Although Shammai declined to reply, his motto was, 'Make the study of the Torah your chief occupation; speak little, but accomplish much; and receive every man with a friendly countenance'.[427] The two are similar: study Scripture and do no harm. This is what the Pharisees thought that it meant to know and follow God.

But the Scriptures, in particular the prophets and the gospels, make it clear that this is not true. Jesus' summary of the law and the prophets is much richer: love God and love your neighbour as God has loved you. Where the Pharisees had only 'study Scripture', Jesus commands a relationship of single-minded devotion to God. Where the Pharisees had 'do no harm' and 'be friendly', Jesus commands forsaking our own needs and necessities to meet those of any needy person we come across, loving them not just as if they were ourselves, but in the same way that Jesus loves us.

Jesus said that our righteousness had to surpass that of

the Pharisees. The Pharisees' righteousness was negative: things that they didn't do; and private: laws like tithing, prayer, and fasting, which rarely require personal contact with others. Jesus' righteousness is positive: things that are to be done; and public: physical interaction with others.

The Pharisees sought purity through rules, but this did not make them pure. Instead, they were 'full of greed and wickedness'[428] despite their earnest attempts to do right. They emphasised prayer and study of Scripture, and were likely instrumental in the creation of the synagogues in which Jesus and the early Christians did much of their preaching. But this did not mean that they knew God. On the outside they looked as though they were right, but on the inside they were not, because they neglected the poor.

PURE AND FAULTLESS RELIGION

The Westminster Catechism says that man's chief and highest end is to glorify God and enjoy him forever. We were made to live lives that bring honour and praise to God, and in which we honour and praise God.

The second commandment tells us that we cannot worship God any way we please. We may only worship God in the way which he lays down for us. And this includes worshipping him in our lives as well as our religious rituals. This ties in to the third commandment, against blasphemy, because attempting to worship only by ritual and not by changed lives is a blasphemy against God. This was a repeated charge of God against his people: not that they stopped the religious rites, but that they stopped the economic and social justice and generosity without which the rites were worse than useless.

The Bible is clear about what God wants from us in the way of religion and relationship with God. God says that pure and faultless religion is to look after orphans and widows in their distress.[429] He says that the fasting that he wants is for you to break the chains of injustice and untie the cords of the yoke; to set the oppressed free and break every yoke; to share your food with the hungry and to provide the poor wanderer with shelter; when you see the naked, to clothe them; and not to turn away from your own flesh and blood.[430] He says that knowing God means to do what is just and right; to rescue from the hand of the oppressor the one who has been robbed; to do no wrong or violence to the foreigner, the fatherless or the widow; to not shed innocent blood; to do what is right and just; and to defend the cause of the poor and needy.[431] How much of that do you do?

All our study of Scripture; all our devotion to religious rituals and behaviours; all our prayer and worship and fasting: all of it is nothing if we do not care – genuinely, with love – for the poor. God says it clearly and repeatedly, and the wonder is how we have missed it for so long:

It is not possible to worship God whilst neglecting the poor. We can perform the outward rites and even think that we have sincere hearts, but if we neglect oppression and injustice then our outward rites are abhorrent to God. Only when we combine right living in all its fullness can we truly worship God, for only then will our lives also proclaim God's glory. To combine wrong living with religious ritual is to defame God by misrepresenting his character to the world, making it look either as though he also does not care about justice, generosity, and holiness or as though he is not worth obeying in what he does command. It is to dishonour him in our lives by making a hypocrisy of the rituals that we do offer.

It's so engrained in us that 'Christian' behaviour is all

the church stuff that we do, or the stuff that we do in the privacy of our homes – Bible reading, prayer, right sexual relationships – that any suggestion we must care for the poor and seek to reverse economic injustice is condemned as 'faith by works'. We struggle to get our head around how it is that we are saved only by Jesus' death in our place on the cross, and not by our own works, and yet we must also work out our salvation.[432]

That we are justified by faith alone and not by works is no excuse for not living holy and just lives. Rather, if we truly understand what God has done for us and want to worship him in response, then we should let that worship spread to the whole of our lives and strive that God may be brought glory in every action that we take.

MORE THAN RELIGION

There is more to religion than studying the Scriptures. Scripture points to God, but it is not God; the goal is not to know Scripture but to know God. It is distressingly easy to lose sight of God in study of his word; to know his word but never know him. It is like studying the life and works of a still-living person, yet never meeting let alone living with them.

Scripture is the rule by which we test all else, but it is not where we stop. It is good to know the Scriptures, but it is good because it is a key aid in knowing and meeting God. Scripture shows us where our emotions and ideas about God are wrong, so that we can truly know him as he is. If we don't know Scripture, then we will end up making our own version of God, at risk of imputing motives and actions and judgments to God that he does not hold. But having known Scripture, we must then act on the knowledge that we have.

The true Christian is one who not just hears God's will

– studies the Scriptures – but obeys it. And the obedience that God wants is that we love him and love others. When we keep within orthodox teaching on marriage, we are loving God by obeying the institution he set in place for sexual activity. We refrain from sexual activity outside of marriage because it would harm the other person as well as ourselves and our current or future marriage partner. This is in keeping with Pharisees' 'do no harm' principle. But Jesus goes beyond the negative, into the positive: we must positively do good.

We can't simply refrain from harm. It isn't enough to say that we don't harm others. It isn't merely that we in developed countries do, in fact, harm others indirectly on a frequent basis through our excessive consumption of the earth's resources and our appetite for cheap prices that are only viable by harming the environment and underpaying and overworking the labourers. It is that we should be actively seeking to do good to others. We should not just refrain from using companies that exploit their staff but should challenge the law that allows such things to happen and actively seek to see labourers be, if anything, overpaid for their labour. We should not just refrain from hurting or ignoring the homeless, but actively work to find them a home and food, and make sure that there are enough homes and jobs for everyone. There is a great deal of intentional direct positivity in how God acts towards us, and the same is expected of his true followers. After all, he has freely given us all things.

In Luke 16:1-9, Jesus uses a parable to commend the shrewdness of non-believers using money to store up favour on earth. His point is that Christians should show the same shrewdness: we should use our money to be generous to those in need, even at cost to ourselves, and

241

so store up favour in heaven. And he then goes on to say, 'if you have not been faithful in the use of that which is another's, who will give you that which is your own?'[433] The money and possessions which we have on earth are not our own: they are God's. God both commands us to use this money for the good of others, and commends those who do so.

SAVING FAITH

This in no way means that our salvation depends upon our works. But a verbal response to God on its own is inadequate. Many people believe in God; indeed, even the demons do. But the demons do not wish to obey God.[434] It is entirely possible to acknowledge God's existence and then deliberately choose your own way, or simply to drift away from God over time. After all, many of the seeds that God scatters do not lead to a harvest; some get eaten by the devil, scorched by hardship, or entangled by wealth.

Again and again in the gospels, Jesus declares who his followers are: not those with the right ideas, but those with the right behaviours. Salvation comes to those who obey God:[435] the good deeds that shine like light;[436] the obedient man who is secure in God;[437] the person who does the will of God;[438] the son who went to the vineyard as his father commanded, even after saying he wouldn't;[439] the shepherd who cared for the needy.[440] Those who obey God become his family. Those who are saved are known by the fruit that they produce: the goodness of their lives and the practical consequences of Spirit-filled love, joy, peace, patience, kindness, goodness, faithfulness, gentleness, and self-control.

Jesus says: It is not enough to call me 'Lord'. Only he who does the will of God will enter heaven.[441] The one who hears my words and obeys them is saved; he who hears and does not obey will be destroyed.[442] He who does the will of God is a child of God.[443] When you show love to your enemies, do good to them, and lend to them without expecting anything back, then you are a child of God.[444]

God tells us that the person who says 'I know God' but does not do what God commands is a liar; he does not know God.[445] Anyone who does not do what is right is not a child of God; nor is anyone who does not love his brother.[446] Words that are not supported by actions are empty, meaningless, and useless; they have no salvific value.[447] We cannot truthfully say we know God if we do not obey God; conversely, we have assurance that we do indeed know God if we obey him.[448] That obedience is shown primarily in our love for the poor and needy: loving our neighbour is how we love God; and loving our neighbour and God is the summation and purpose of all the law and the prophets.

Faith is not a verbal assent to God, but a changed life that gives loyalty, honour, and obedience to God. It is not enough to say that salvation is through Jesus alone if we then ignore or reject that salvation through a lack of repentance for our sins. And repentance doesn't mean remorse; it means changing our behaviour. We have to stop committing the sins of the past and start obeying God's commands. If we are not now obeying God, then our behaviour hasn't changed, and our verbal assent that God is God is worthless. We are like people who say 'Lord, Lord', and even cast out demons and heal the sick in Jesus' name, but whom Jesus never knew.[449] We can say the right things and invoke God's power and still not have the repentance and love that God requires.

Ultimately, what God wants from us is not just the

outward honour of ritual. We must have the inward honour of changed lives that results in outward actions to the good of others. Only when we serve those in need are we able to truly, honestly, and wholeheartedly worship God in the way that he deserves and desires.

CARING FOR THE POOR

When God declares his care for the poor, he does not mean his concern for the spiritually poor. God also expresses concern for these people, but in a different way: he declares his desire that no-one perish and that all people turn to him for salvation. In contrast, when God says that he defends the cause of the fatherless and the widow and that he loves the alien,[450] he is talking about the literally orphaned, bereaved, and stateless. It is what he did in rescuing the Israelites. When Hannah declares that God raises the poor and lifts the needy,[451] she is referring to people in physical poverty. Similarly, when God gives commands that his people seek justice, encourage the oppressed, defend the cause of the fatherless, and plead the case of the widow,[452] he means that we are to ensure justice for and defend the cause of the physically poor and powerless. And when he says that defending the poor and needy is what it means to know God,[453] he means that those who know God care practically for the physically poor, and that those who care practically for the physically poor know God.

God identifies with the poor. How we treat the poor is how we treat God. Whoever oppresses the poor shows contempt for their Maker, but whoever is kind to the needy honours God.[454] Whoever is kind to the poor lends to God.[455] Whoever feeds the hungry, gives water to the thirsty, invites the stranger into their home, gives clothes to those in need, looks after those who are sick, and visits those in prison does all those things to God. Whoever neglects those things turns away from God.[456]

To those who engage in the religious disciplines without caring for the poor, God says, 'You cannot fast as you do today and expect your voice to be heard by me.[457] If you shut your ears to the cries of the poor, I will shut my ears to you..'[458] If Amos were writing today, he might say: 'I hate, I despise your Easter and Christmas celebrations; your church meetings are a stench to me. I will not accept your tithes or give any regard to your service in church. Away with your songs of worship! I will not listen to them.'[459]

When Jesus is asked what it means to love our neighbour, he replies that it means to help physically, practically, those who are in physical and material need, starting with the nearest. And given that this is the second greatest commandment, on which together with the commandment to love God hangs all of the law and the prophets, this is pretty important. John explains that we cannot love God if we do not love others; if we love God, then we love others; if we love God, then we practically and physically help people in need of practical, physical help. It is that simple. Practical action to help the poor and needy is what it means to know God, what it means to serve God, what it means to love God, and it is the marker of true religion.

God says that we cannot love him if we do not love others. When asked what that love looks like, God gave the parable of the Good Samaritan as his answer. Loving God is loving people in need. True religion is caring for those in need. Knowing God is caring for those in need. Ministering to God is ministering to people in need. If we don't care for those in need, then we don't know God.

We don't love him and, by implication, we do not have a saving faith. This is serious.

Caring for the poor is a major part of Christianity. It was not beneath God, and is not beneath us either. Sitting on a hillside, facing 5,000 people whom he had crossed a lake to avoid and then spent hours teaching, Jesus didn't say that it was beneath his ministry or deity to minister to something so basic as physical needs. He had sought time alone with his disciples, but when people turned up seeking him he did not turn them away. He fed them and cared for them, even though they had come to him for many wrong reasons. This is, therefore, how God expects us to behave.

Christians are commanded that love always trusts and does not store up a record of wrongs. This means that love would not use someone's past failures as an excuse not to help them in their need, for that would be to use records of wrongs against someone in their present need, and to refuse to show them the grace that Christ has shown us. It also means that love would not assume that a person who is poor is morally defective in some way, because that would be to refuse to trust that they have good in them when we know that everyone, whilst sinful, is made in the image of God; it would be to judge someone guilty without even a semblance of a fair investigation of the truth; and it would be to assume that all that is needed to overcome a poor education, limited access to timely and quality healthcare, time-consuming commutes to work, caring duties for family or one's own ill-health, a housing shortage that causes high housing costs, an insufficiency of jobs that means labourers at the bottom compete for employment rather than employers competing for employees, and general deprivation of poor areas is: the 'right attitude'.

Love doesn't blame people for external situations, expect them to overcome substantial barriers and difficulties by themselves, or hold past mistakes as a reason to refuse to help. Love doesn't use current failures as a reason to withhold necessary support.

This is not to say that people in poverty do not at times make decisions that contribute to their hardship. But it is to say that primarily changing these decisions will not lift people out of poverty. Even drug addicts and criminals, who might be considered to have most contributed to their own poverty, nevertheless cannot be expected to get themselves out of it on their own, if only because the majority of the world will not employ a self-confessed addict or criminal. They need prolonged practical and relational support; they need to be offered the opportunity to work, and the help to sustain it. They need to be given a secure and stable life so that they are not put in situations where the temptation to relapse overwhelms them, because of the stress and misery of their day-to-day life.

Never eating chocolate will not save one enough money to buy a house. Never enjoying a treat or a day-out will not give one access to a better paying job. Denying yourself anything that makes life worth living won't end bad working conditions or move a job closer to your home. Refusing to buy your children any gifts at Christmas won't help them enjoy, and do better in, school. Never letting your child participate on an equal footing with their peers won't give them a self-esteem or morale boost to improve their education and learning. Reinforcing their low social standing through your spending choices won't help their health.

We should show the same grace to the poor that God shows to us. We are all steeped in sin; utterly unable to pull ourselves out of the pit into which we have freely chosen to go; completely undeserving of any help or reward. Yet God goes very far out of his way to pull us out of our own mess. He doesn't wait for signs that we regret our choices or repent of some of our wrong deeds. He doesn't wait for indications that we are trying, however futilely, to get out of the situation we have put ourselves into. He doesn't ask the extent to which our problem is our fault. Instead, he comes freely, before many of us were even born, to offer a grace that many would have never asked for, to reconcile us to himself when it was our choice to be estranged in the first place. What would such grace extended to the poor look like?

No-one is perfect. There are changes that people in poverty can make that might lead to better outcomes (depending on time-scales, other factors, and personal weightings of what is better), or mistakes they've made that they wish they hadn't. We should challenge sin, especially amongst Christians. But our knowledge of human sinfulness ought to make us more sympathetic to the poor, not less. It ought to make us more willing to ensure that poor people have access to a home and work and society, not less. Our understanding of our own sinfulness ought to make us more generous and more ready to give without judgment or conditions, because we know what grace and mercy have meant and how they have protected and helped us when shown to us. We should understand our own failures and how it has been access to money, family, and other resources that protected us from harm, not an absence of failure or mistakes. Even the apostle Paul, perhaps one of the godliest Christians to have ever lived, complains that the good he wants to do he does not do, and the bad he does not want to do he does do. And this is Paul, a highly educated man filled with the Holy Spirit.

Why then do we blame poor people, who do not have God, for failing to be perfect? Why do we make help contingent upon their behaviour, when God has never made his support for us contingent on our good deeds? Why do we assume that we don't need to step in to ensure justice unless the person we're helping has never done anything wrong? Why are we so afraid of showing others the grace that God has shown us?

Is it that we see in ourselves our own failure to respond appropriately to God's grace, so we fear that others also won't respond well to grace? Is our own sinfulness in the face of God's mercy being used to claim that it's okay to be unjust and ungenerous, on the assumption that the person we help won't respond perfectly either? Perhaps our refusal to help the poor is not because they are sinful, but because we know how ungratefully we often behave towards what God has given us. Perhaps we can't imagine that they will behave better if we are just and generous to them. Our hearts are hard and arrogant, and we use that to self-justify further sin.

No-one is perfect. But the fact is that poverty is not primarily a fault of the poor, and when we blame the poor we become rogues who slander the poor in order to deny them justice and a decent living standard.[460] The fact is that what the poor need is not education on how to do better or telling off for doing wrong. They need the grace that all Christians have been shown by God, and are commanded to extend to others. They need the access to resources that God intends them to have. They need a fair, just, and dramatically more equal society than is currently seen in the UK. They need Christians to act like Christ.

SEEKING JUSTICE

Michael Sandel, professor of political philosophy at Harvard University, outlines three components of social justice: maximising welfare; promoting freedom; and rewarding virtue.[461] Which of these you prioritise has substantial impacts on the policies you favour and the approach you take to addressing poverty. The problem with all of them is that they tend to end up favouring the rich over the poor; the healthy over the sick and disabled; the multiply-lucky over the profoundly unlucky.

Promoting freedom

For the economist Milton Friedman, 'freedom' was an ultimate goal. Friedman claimed that 'A society that puts equality – in the sense of equality of outcome – ahead of freedom will end up with neither equality nor freedom.... On the other hand, a society that puts freedom first will, as a happy by-product, end up with both greater freedom and greater equality.'[462] It's a great statement that merits investigation to test whether or not it is true. There is no particular reason to believe that it is true – sounding good is not the same as being right.

The first problem for Friedman is that the Bible is full of constraints on individual freedom. If you have an infectious disease, you are isolated from your community; if your house contains an aggressive mould, the entirety of it has to be pulled down. If your family member is poor, you are commanded to buy back any property he has had to sell; if a neighbour is poor, you are required to help her. You aren't allowed to scrape up all the profit of your work or your business to yourself but are constrained to leave enough to support the poor. You are required to help your enemy when his animal is in trouble and to send off your servants after six years' labour with a generous golden farewell.

God's idea of justice and right-ness includes putting constraints on the freedom of the high-earners to keep that wealth to themselves. He even constrains the ability to earn, by placing limits on business practices and banning any profit derived from lending money or selling necessities to the poor. Friedman condemned the idea that businesses should have a 'social conscience' and take seriously their 'responsibilities for providing employment, eliminating discrimination, avoiding pollution' and so on.[463] God heavily constrained the freedom to accrue wealth and made clear laws regarding employment, the care of the land, and support for poor people. This tells us that freedom does not lead to equality, as Friedman thought; if Friedman were right, God would not have needed to constrain the ability of individual Israelites to grow rich.

The second problem for Friedman is that the evidence shows that putting individual freedom first does not result in both greater freedom and greater equality. The freedom of the rich and powerful to keep their wealth and power means that they accrue more and more, in both absolute and relative terms. Poorer people end up priced out of necessary goods such as housing, because richer people easily out-bid them. Poorer people end up having their needs disregarded, because richer people can attract the best doctors and teachers to themselves and their children. Poorer people see their local areas go under-invested, because richer people find it easier to buy the ears and favour of policy makers for practices that favour the rich to the detriment of the poor rather than vice versa. Freedom for the rich necessarily means a loss of freedom

– deprivation, oppression, exploitation, even enslavement – for the poor, because a lack of money and resources means a lack of power; and a lack of power means a lack of freedom; and all of this means a loss of opportunity and a fall in social mobility.

If your focus is on promoting freedom, then you dislike placing restrictions on what people can do; and in the balance between your right to do what you want and my right for your actions not to harm me, you will be closer to your right to do what you want. You will be happier with a greater harm to other people because you think that it is itself a major harm to have your freedom restricted. During the COVID-19 pandemic, you were probably against any compulsion to wear face masks or be vaccinated – your freedom to choose whether or not you (unintentionally, if you have pre- or a- symptomatic COVID) breathe out infected air into other people's breathing space overrode their freedom to breathe uninfected air whilst in common shared spaces such as supermarkets or churches. You may have been against the ban on smoking indoors in shared spaces, and against the law making it compulsory to wear seat-belts in cars in the UK.

The problem with this approach is that it assumes equal freedom: you can just as easily choose to avoid areas polluted by my germs or cigarette smoke as I can choose to pollute the areas you want to use. But my freedom to go maskless in a supermarket, spreading germs, is not equalled by your freedom to find supermarkets that don't allow unmasked people: supermarkets don't offer two versions of everything, one in an area where people can enter without masks and one in an area (with a different air circulation) where only people wearing masks can enter.

Another example where personal freedom comes

up against harm to others is in abortion. This time, advocates of personal freedom tend to be on the political left, whilst the conservative right champion the rights of the vulnerable to not be harmed. On the side of personal freedom, the argument is that it is the woman's body and her right to choose: the dependence of another life on her body does not mean that the woman has to temporarily devote her body to that life, and the right to life in general does not include the right to use another person's body. Therefore, the woman is free to choose whether or not to support a life within her body. On the side of protecting the vulnerable, every human has equal value right from the moment of conception, and the harm to the baby is so severe and certain relative to the harm to the woman that it overrides the woman's right to choose. After all, my right to use my body to pull the trigger on a loaded gun depends in large part upon what I am aiming at: I may not use my body to commit murder or damage another person's property.

Another issue at the moment is the freedom of businesses to pollute the environment: the freedom to release CO_2, methane, sulphur dioxide, nitrogen oxides and other polluting gases into the atmosphere; the freedom to dump raw sewage in our rivers and seas; the freedom to cut down trees, drain wetlands, plough up soil, add chemicals, and destroy soil structure, biodiversity, and the ecological network; the freedom to produce products with short lifespans and polluting components. This is promoting the freedom of the company to make a profit without adequate regard for the consequences on other people. We have yet to find an effective way to 'internalise' the externalities of these costs to the businesses and people who create them.

The same issue holds true across multiple areas: people who are vulnerable to the consequences of the personal freedom of others tend to be the poorest and least able to mitigate that vulnerability. These people typically have less political power, and are less able to influence policy decisions in their favour. The consequence is policies that favour the better-off over the poor; the powerful over the powerless; the strong over the vulnerable. There is an inherent tendency therefore in politics for policies to favour personal freedom at excessive cost to others. Maximising freedom is a bad way to run a country because it harms the poorer and less powerful.

Rewarding virtue

If your focus is on rewarding virtue, then a typical policy goal is to reduce taxes on the better-off in order to allow them to keep more of their income as a reward for their effort. This of course assumes that incomes are already proportionate to a person's effort or the true value of their work to society – something which was briefly highlighted during the COVID pandemic, as it became clear that many of the most valuable workers in society were the least well-paid and endured the worst working conditions. Rewarding virtue therefore requires a substantial effort to determine what are the works that we want to see rewarded – are cleaners less important to a functioning society than financial speculators, for example? And this also requires substantial regulation in order to enforce appropriate incomes for many currently low-paid professions whilst restricting the excessive wages of others.

But the reward of virtue faces another problem: it assumes that any given act of virtue is equally easy (or hard) to perform for everyone. And yet this is manifestly untrue. A typical single jobseeker in the UK receives a little under £91/week for living costs, and has to contribute some of that towards rent and council tax, when the threshold for destitution – the ability to afford the bare necessities – is £95/week.[464] Are you really going to insist that it is just as easy for this person not to steal a bar of chocolate as it is for someone earning more than they need? Are you going to claim that it is just as easy for them to refrain from engaging in cash-in-hand work as it is for a wealthy person to refrain from tax-dodging? If this person loses his temper with the staff at the Jobcentre, are you going to place as much blame on them as you do on the well-paid manager who loses her temper with her staff?

It is harder to be virtuous when you are financially poor, time poor, cold, hungry, tired, stressed, and distressed. It is also harder to be rewarded for your virtue. If you are in a job that has career progression, you may be rewarded for good work by a pay rise or promotion. If you are in an entry-level job or looking for work, the reward for your hard effort is to not get sacked or sanctioned. Virtue is not just harder when your circumstances are harder, it is also less likely to be rewarded – and failures are more likely to be punished.

Nor is rewarding virtue the approach that God takes whilst we're still on this earth. God's approach is to extend mercy and grace: to refrain from giving us our just punishment, and to choose instead to give us good things which we have not earned. This is the God who left the 99 sheep to find the one;[465] who gave the elder brother's fatted calf to the spendthrift younger brother;[466] and who paid those who had worked one hour in the cool of the day the same amount as those who had worked all day and during the heat of the day.[467] This is a gracious God whose desire is to have mercy.

If we do want society to reward virtue, then we are going to have to do a much better job of determining exactly what work or virtue merits what level of reward. But we are also going to have to deal with the question of forgiveness, grace, and mercy. If God treated us according to our virtue, we would all be going straight to hell.

Maximising welfare

If you are interested in maximising welfare, an interesting question arises as to how to do that. What is the value of human life generally? What is the value of any given human life?

At a meeting with economists, Sir Michael Marmot presented data showing that higher-ranked members of the UK civil service had better health. Marmot argued that if two members had renal failure, with one in a higher-paid position than the other, then both had equal right to dialysis or transplant. The economists, he said 'disputed that, vigorously and all at once.'[468] They said that the higher-ranked person should be prioritised for dialysis or transplant. Michael Marmot explains that 'if you use the valuation of life to make allocation decisions, you spend money where it will yield the greatest result, measured in dollars. It is inefficient to care for the poor, the sick and the young.'

This approach – maximising welfare – actually perpetuates inequality. It means that wealthier people should get better healthcare because they are likely to receive a greater benefit from any given level of healthcare. Their overall better health, greater wealth, and higher status in society means they are likely to live longer and be returned to a higher level of health following any given intervention than a person of lower health. But this merely exacerbates existing inequality in fortune. Most wealthy, healthy people are people who were born to richer parents in richer countries and benefited from all that this brings in terms of better education, health, and extra-curricular activities as children – all factors outside of their personal control. These factors then give them access to higher-status jobs with higher pay, better working conditions, more autonomy, and a better work-life balance. They are already benefiting from a lot of luck in life, right from the place, parents, and time of birth. To then say that these are the people who should be prioritised for healthcare or other welfare-promoting policies is to perpetuate the inequality and unfairness of life.

Promoting the welfare of the poor

Here is what I suggest the laws that God gave to the Israelites resulted in: promoting the welfare of the poor.

When it comes to preserving the freedom of the rich to keep their money, God says they must give freely to the poor; cancel debt after seven years; never take essential items in pledge; always leave food available; pay workers daily and fairly; not impose hard working conditions; and send workers away with a generous golden farewell. The wealthy person who has purchased another person's land or home cannot keep it forever, but only for a maximum of 49 years, after which it returns to the original owner. God does not preserve individual freedom if others are in poverty or suffering. The right of the vulnerable to protection over-rides the right of the rich to personal freedom. When it comes to property, the right that concerns God is the right of the poor to retain ultimate ownership of house, land, and access to work.

When it comes to rewarding virtue, God says that it is the workers – not the business owners – who are to benefit. It is their pay, working conditions, access to necessities, and ability to accrue savings that is to be protected. The poor must be helped generously, regardless of the reason for their poverty (which is never mentioned in the Old Testament laws) or their ability to repay – indeed, factoring in a person's ability to pay when considering whether or not to lend money is strictly forbidden as a wicked act. Furthermore, every person must remember that all that they have is from God as an act of grace. None of us deserves any good thing in our lives, given our sinfulness; we therefore cannot claim anything as a reward for our personal virtue.

When it comes to maximising welfare, God forbids favouritism. The rich must not be prioritised over the poor. All must be treated with equal fairness before the law. Everyone has equal right – given to us by God and not by virtue – to the necessities of life and to participation in social life. But justice does not mean protecting the excess property of the middle class, never mind the ultra-rich.

There are problems with focusing on freedom, virtue, or utilitarian calculations of maximising welfare. All of them end up favouring the rich over the poor, the powerful over the powerless, the decision makers over the decision-receivers. And none of them measure up to God's requirement, which is that we focus on generosity and justice in order to raise the welfare of the poor, even if it is at the cost of the rich. None of them match up to the way God treats us.

Our God is a power-sharing, others-loving, gracious, and merciful God. When God came to live on earth, he wasn't promoting the virtuous but rather the unvirtuous.

He said that he came to save sinners; that he was here for the worst people, just like a doctor comes for the sick and not for the healthy.[469] He said that the one who loves much is the one who has experienced much love; that people who have been forgiven the most – i.e., those who had sinned the most – become the most loving and forgiving, because of what they have received.[470] More grace and mercy is shown to worse sinners.

When Jesus came to earth, he didn't champion personal freedom. The only freedom he was interested in was the freedom to do good to others. So he healed on the Sabbath, despite the Sabbath restrictions, because it is right to do good. He taught the people and fed the hungry, even though he was tired himself. He got up early to pray, rather than insist on his personal freedom and right to a 'quiet time' with God at a convenient hour. He came to serve rather than to be served; and to give his life rather than save his life. He gave up all his right to the glories of heaven and exchanged them for life as a manual worker and itinerant preacher. Jesus' life was all about other people and nothing about his own rights and freedoms.

When Jesus walked on earth, he cared about everyone who came to him for help. But that didn't stop him castigating the elite for the burdens they placed on other people and their failure to help those in need. When he healed people, he didn't factor in a utilitarian calculation as to whether this person's health was more valuable than another's. When he was on his way to a dying child, he stopped to heal a bleeding woman, even though that child then died. He insisted that the little children be allowed to come to him, even though they weren't important people. He ate with tax collectors and prostitutes and sinners, even though that demeaned him in the eyes of the religious leaders. He told a parable of leaving 99 sheep in an open field – vulnerable to wolves – in order to find and rescue one lost sheep. He told another parable of welcoming a disloyal son home with a feast, at the cost of the loyal son to whom the fatted calf belonged. Jesus didn't make utilitarian calculations that said it made more sense to favour the rich and powerful. He refused the economics of power, and spent his life amongst the poor and the despised.

God's way is always the way that seems to be of weakness. It is the way of humility, of forsaking one's own 'rights', of seeking the good of others, and of standing up for the poor and oppressed. It is the way of maximising the welfare of the lowest people in society, and raising others up even if it means lowering ourselves. It is the way that champions the rights and needs of the poor.

CONCLUSION

As Christians, we should seek with the entirety of our lives – with all our heart, soul, mind, and strength – to honour, worship, and bring glory to God. Our money, our possessions, and our energy should all be devoted to this purpose. Every action we take should work towards this goal. This includes the way we live at home; our purchasing and consumption choices; our treatment of people over whom we have authority; and our actions towards a just society. If we don't do this, then it hampers our worship of God, to the point of making our worship nothing more than a stench to God and rebellious idolatry in his eyes.

This is not merely a question of personal piety and individual charity. It is also about how we live in community; in the society in which we are placed; with the resources and responsibilities which God has given us. It includes a prophetic role, to hold not just ourselves but other people – and in particular those with power and influence – to account for the sort of society that we create. This means that we need to consider what God says a just society looks like, and having established those principles we need to also think about how they are best put into practice.

It is my suggestion, in this book, that in developed countries the government has a major role in working to set up a society in which everyone has access to a home, work, income, and support for key needs such as healthcare and education. In other countries, where governments have less trust and capacity for action, there may be a greater need for charity to fill the gap created by the failure to set up a just society. But this does not mean that developed countries can ignore the fact that God did give his people a form of government with rules that regulated business practice and the structure of society. Furthermore, that society is one where the underlying principle is to promote the wellbeing of the poor, and the laws that are established to govern society are set up to achieve that end.

For Christians, these are not optional questions. Defending the poor and needy is a core part of who God is, and should therefore be a core part of Christian life. We need to know what are the issues facing poor people as well as what can be done to prevent and alleviate poverty. We need to be willing to take personal action to help people in need, through acts of generosity and charity. But that is not enough. Charity is not the same as defending the poor. We need to also be willing to tell our leaders what God says on these matters, and hold them to account for how they run the country. And if we are in a position of power

261

ourselves – perhaps as a business leader or a politician – then we need to work to bring about a just country.

Christianity is not just about our individual, private lives but also about how we live and interact in society to work with others to achieve justice according to God's definition. And when we do finally bring every part of our lives into line with God's will and character, that is when we truly worship and honour him.

ENDNOTES

INTRODUCTION

1   Homer, *The Odyssey*, as translated by E. V. Rieu (1949) https://archive.org/stream/in.ernet.dli.2015.59061/2015.59061.Homer-The-Odyssey_djvu.txt

2   E.g.,https://www.reddit.com/r/DebateReligion/comments/ 8j1ymz/religion_has_no_place_in_politics/

3   Dowler, S. (12/09/2017), 'Religion has no place in politics and never will', *Huffington Post*

4   Duthie, R. (18/09/2017), 'Rees-Mogg is wrong, religion has no place in politics', *Cherwell*

5   Scott, A. (10/06/2021), 'No place for God in British politics', *Politico.*

6   Killerman, S (2012), 'I'm not anti-Christian, but religion shouldn't have a place in political decisions', https://www.itspronouncedmetrosexual.com/

7   I come from a traditional Protestant tradition which includes 'sola scriptura' and taking the Bible as our authority on matters of salvation, orthodoxy, and orthopraxy. It is from this position that this book is written.

8   Solzhenitsyn, A. (1973), *The Gulag Archipelago 1918-1956.*

263

9   O'Donovan, O (2013), *Self, World and Time: Ethics as Theology 1* (Grand Rapids: Eerdmans Publishing Co), pp. 79-80

10 Witt, W. (19/06/2020), *Response to the Anglican Diocese of the Living Word: Hermeneutics and Complementarianism*, blog: willgwitt.org.

CHAPTER 1: WHY WE WORSHIP GOD

11 Matthew 26:13

12 From Matthew 5:16 NIV: 'In the same way, let your light shine before others, that they may see your good deeds and glorify your Father in heaven.'

13 Deuteronomy 10:21

14 1 Chronicles 16:28-29

15 Ephesians 5:19-20

16 Exodus 3:13-15

17 Daniel 2:20

18 Psalm 8:1

19 Psalm 145:3

20 Ephesians 3:20

21 Psalm 19

22 Isaiah 40:26

23 Isaiah 6:3; Revelation 4:8

24 Deuteronomy 10:18; Psalm 140:12

25 Psalm 146:7

26 Deuteronomy 32:4; Job 8:3; Psalm 7:11, 36:6

27 Psalm 136:26

28 John 3:16; Romans 5:8; Ephesians 2:4-5

29 Romans 8:37-39

30 2 Thessalonians 1:9

31 Matthew 13:50

32 Revelation 21:3-4

33 1 Corinthians 15:35-55

34 Revelation 21:9-21; 22:1-2

35 Exodus 16

36 Isaiah 57:1

37 John 9:3

38 Deuteronomy 10:16, 20-21a

39 1 Chronicles 8-10, 23-25, 28-29

40 John 4:23

41 John 2:21

42 1 Kings 12:28-30

43 John 3:21

CHAPTER 2: HOW WE WORSHIP GOD: BLASPHEMY AND IDOLATRY

44 *The Uncommon Truth at The Father's House Church,* Oroville, California

45 Ehrman, M. (26/10/2020), 'Accomplishing God's plan in your community', *The Uncommon Truth* 73 (Oroville, California: Father's House Church)

46 See e.g. Leviticus 24:11; 2 Chronicles 32:9-19; Acts 26:11

47 2 Peter 2:1

48 2 Peter 2:18

49 Numbers 15:30

50 Isaiah 52:5

51 Ezekiel 36:20

52 Ezekiel 20:27

53 Calvin, J. (1536), Institutes of the Christian religion

54 Romans 12:1

55 John 15:8

56 John 15:10

57 Matthew 5:16

58 1 Peter 2:12

59 1 Timothy 2:9-10

60 Piper, J. (03/08/1980), 'How to do good so that God gets the glory' https://www.desiringgod.org/messages/how-to-do-good-so-that-god-gets-the-glory

61 Titus 2:14

62 Ephesians 2:10

63 Piper, J. (03/08/1980), 'How to do good so that God gets the glory' https://www.desiringgod.org/messages/how-to-do-good-so-that-god-gets-the-glory

64 1 Corinthians 13:3

65 Matthew 7:22-23

66 1 Peter 4:10-11

67 1 Corinthians 10:31

68 Ephesians 6:7

69 Colossians 3:23

70 Piper, J. (03/08/1980), 'How to do good so that God gets the glory' https://www.desiringgod.org/messages/how-to-do-good-so-that-god-gets-the-glory

71 Abbott, S. (19/03/2021), Alister McGrath on John Polkinghorne, Shelby Abbott on doubt and Mark Clark on Jesus, *Unbelievable?* podcast with Justin Brierley

72 Bowers, J. (22/07/2019), 'No more Mr Nice Jesus' with Johnny Bowers, *The Uncommon Truth 015* (Oroville, California: The Father's House Church)

73 Matthew 7:21

74 John 8:51

75 John 12:26

76 Matthew 7:24; Luke 6:46-48

77 John 8:39

78 Matthew 12:50; Mark 3:35

79 Luke 8:15

80 Luke 11:28

81 John 13:13-17

82 Luke 12:47-48; John 12:47-48.

83 John 8:34-36

84 Luke 11:23

85 John 5:44

86 John 8:47; 10:4-5, 16, 26-27, 33

87 Luke 11:35

88 John 3:21

89 John 18:37

CHAPTER 3: GOD'S CITIZENS: FULFILLING GOD'S LAW

90 Zaklikowski, D., *Maimonides: His Life and Works*, Chabad.org https://www.chabad.org/library/article_ cdo/aid/75991/jewish/Maimonides-His-Life-and-Works.htm

91 E.g. as in Booth, P. (2009), 'Government, solidarity and subsidiarity' in *God and Government*, Spencer, N. and Chaplin, J. (eds.) (London: SPCK)

92 Deuteronomy 22:8

93 Deuteronomy 22:8

94 Deuteronomy 25:12

95 Exodus 21:29

96 1 Corinthians 6:18

97 Aquinas, *Summa Theologica, Prima Secundae Partis*, Question 96, The power of human law

98 McIlroy, D. (201), 'Government in classical Christian political thought', in *God and Government*, Spencer, N. and Chaplin, J. (eds) (London: SPCK), p. 101

99 Martens, M. (02/08/2022), 'Government's two-edged sword' (Providence: providencemag.com)

100 As cited by McIlroy, D. (201), 'Government in classical Christian political thought', in *God and Government*, Spencer, N. and Chaplin, J. (eds.) (London: SPCK), p. 87

101 Book 4, Chapter 4, *The City of God* as cited by McIlroy, D. (201) 'Government in classical Christian political thought', in *God and Government*, Spencer, N. and Chaplin, J. (eds.) (London: SPCK), p. 97

102 Padley, M. and Stone, J. (2021), 'Households below the Minimum Income Standard: 2008-2021' (York: Joseph Rowntree Foundation)

103 BBC Reality Check (07/02/2018) 'Reality Check: What has happened to police numbers?'

104 Cox, G. (23/01/2019), speaking to the House of Commons Justice Committee

105 Hyde, J. (27/04/2022), '£1bn courts repair bill is threat to justice system, MPs report', The Law Society Gazette

106 Law Centres Network (September 2018), LASPO Act 2012 Post-Implementation Review 4.

107 The Bar Council (2020), Bar Council Spending Review Submission, September 2020

108 Quote and figures taken from the Social Mobility Commission 2019

CHAPTER 4: GOD'S SOCIETY: AMASSING WEALTH

109 Mischel W. Ebbesen EB and Raskoff, Zeiss A. (1972), 'Cognitive and attentional mechanisms in delay of gratification', *Journal of Personality and Social Psychology*, 21(2), 204–218. Doi: 10.1037/h0032198

110 See e.g. Mischel W. Shoda Y. and Peake P. K. (1988), 'The nature of adolescent competencies predicted by

preschool delay of gratification', *Journal of Personality and Social Psychology*, 54(4), 687–696. Doi: 10.1037/0022-3514.54.4.687

Mischel W. Shoda Y. and Rodriguez, M. L. (1989), 'Delay of Gratification in Children'
Science 244(4907):933-938. Doi: 10.1126/science.2658056

Shoda Y. Mischel S. and Peake, P. K. (1990), 'Predicting adolescent cognitive and self-regulatory competencies from preschool delay of gratification: Identifying diagnostic conditions', Developmental Psychology, 26(6), 978-986. Doi: 10.1037/0012-1649.26.6.978

Schlam, T. R., Wilson, N. L., Shoda, Y., Mischel, W. and Ayduk, O. (2013), 'Preschoolers' Delay of Gratification Predicts their Body Mass 30 Years Later', *The Journal of Pediatrics* 162(1):90-93 doi: 10.1016/j.jpeds.2012.06.049

111 Watts, T., Duncan, G. J. and Quan, H. (2018), 'Revisiting the Marshmallow Test: A Conceptual Replication Investigating Links Between Early Delay of Gratification and Later Outcomes', *Psychological Science* 29(7) doi: 10.1177/0956797618761661

112 Kidd, C., Palmeri, H. and Aslin, R. N. (2013), 'Rational snacking: Young children's decision-making on the marshmallow task is moderated by beliefs about environmental reliability', *Cognition* 126(1):109-114 doi: 10.1016/j.cognition.2012.08.004

Michaelson, L. E. and Munakata, Y. (2016), 'Trust matters: Seeing how an adult treats another person influences preschoolers' willingness to delay gratification', *Developmental Science* 19(6):1011-1019 doi: 10.1111/desc.12388

113 Ma, F., Chen, B., Xu, F., Lee, K. and Heyman, G. D. (2018), 'Generalized trust predicts young

children's willingness to delay gratification', *Journal of Experimental Child Psychology* 169:118-125
doi: 10.1016/j.jecp.2017.12.015
More reading: https://effectiviology.com/stanford-marshmallow-experiment-self-control-willpower/

114 Micah 3:11

115 Micah 6:10-11

116 Micah 7:3

117 Micah 3:2-3

118 James 5:3

119 James 5:5

120 Piff, P. (2013), 'Does money make you mean?', TED Talk
See also Gross, J. (20/12/2013), 'Six studies on how money affects the mind', TED Blog

121 Piff, P., Stancato, S., Cote, S., Mendoza-Denton, R. and Keltern, D. (2012), 'Higher social class predicts increased unethical behaviour'. PNAS 109:4086-4091
doi: 10.1073/pnas.1118373109

122 Jeremiah 17:9

123 Luke 16:11-12

124 Psalm 50:11-12; 74:16-17; Nehemiah 9:7; Haggai 2:8

125 Leviticus 25:23

126 Luke 6:38

127 Johnson, B. (27/11/2013), 'What would Maggie do today?' (London: Centre for Policy Studies), Margaret Thatcher Lecture

128 The Harwood Group (1995), 'Yearning for Balance: Views of Americans on Consumption, Materialism, and the Environment'

129 Berg, A. G. and Ostry, J. D. (2011), 'Inequality and unsustainable growth: two sides of the same coin?', Staff Discussion Note SDN/11/08 (Washington:

International Monetary Fund); Ostry J.D., Berg, A.G. and Tsangarides, C. (2014), 'Income distribution, inequality and growth', Staff Discussion Note SDN/14/02 (Washington: International Monetary Fund)

130 Cingano, F. (2014), 'Trends in income inequality and its impact on economic growth', OECD social, employment and migration working papers no. 163, DELSA/ELSA/WD/SEM(2014)9

131 UN (2013), 'The Rise of the South: Human Progress in a Diverse World', Human Development Report 2013.

132 Lundberg, O., Yngwe M.Å., Stjärne, M.K., Björk, L.S. and Fritzell, J. (2008), 'The Nordic Experience: Welfare States and Public Health' (NEWS), Health Equities Studies 12

133 Wilkinson, R. and Pickett, K. (2010), *The Spirit Level: Why more equality is better for everyone*, (London: Penguin).

134 Ibid.

135 Ibid.

136 Ibid. p. 315

137 Ibid.

138 Ibid. pp. 150, 151

139 Marmot, M. (2015), *The Health Gap: the challenge of an unequal world* (London: Bloomsbury Publishing), p. 7

140 Ibid, pp. 62-6

141 Green, F. (2008), 'Work effort and worker well-being in the age of affluence', in Cooper, C. and Burke R. (eds.), 'The long work hours culture: causes, consequences and choices' (Bradford: Emerald Group Publications); Baumberg, B. (2014), 'Fit-for-work – or work fit for disabled people? The role of changing job

demands and control in incapacity claims', *Journal of Social Policy*, Vol 43 Iss. 2, pp. 289-310 doi: 10.1017/S0047279413000810

142 Marmot, M. (2015), *The Health Gap: the challenge of an unequal world* (London: Bloomsbury Publishing), p. 173

143 Ibid.

144 Wilkinson and Pickett (2010), *The Spirit Level: Why more equality is better for everyone* (London: Penguin), p. 322

145 Wilkinson and Pickett (2010), *The Spirit Level: Why more equality is better for everyone* (London: Penguin), p. 323

146 Wilkinson and Pickett (2010) *The Spirit Level: Why more equality is better for everyone.*

147 World Economic Forum (2020) The Global Social Mobility Report 2020: Equality, Opportunity and a New Economic Imperative

148 Marmot, M. (2015), *The Health Gap: the challenge of an unequal world* (London: Bloomsbury Publishing)

CHAPTER 5: GOD'S PEOPLE: THE RICH PATRIARCHS

149 Orsillo, S. (13/04/2020), 'What Jesus says about selflessness'. The Uncommon Truth 045 (Oroville, California: The Father's House Church)

150 Ibid.

151 Orsillo, S. (17/06/2019), 'The definition of a disciple'. The Uncommon Truth 010 (Oroville, California: The Father's House Church)

152 Blomberg, C (1997) Neither Poverty nor Riches (Westmont, Illinois: IVP Academic), pp. 36-7

153 ADHB (2018) UK cattle yearbook, Department of Agriculture and Food (2017), The Western Australian sheep industry, Government of Western Australia.

154 Job 1:1, 3

155 Job 29:7-11; 21-25

156 Job 31:13, 39

157 Job 31:1, 9-12

158 Job 29

159 Job 31:16-23

160 Job 31:24-28

161 Job 1:21

162 Job 1:22

163 Genesis 13:2

164 Genesis 26:7

165 Genesis 26:8-9

166 Genesis 26:22

167 Deuteronomy 17:18; see also 14-20

168 Orsillo, S. (29/06/2020), 'The blueprint for real world change', The Uncommon Truth 056 (Oroville, California: The Father's House Church)

169 Orsillo, S. (02/09/2019), 'Relating to Jesus: doing vs being', The Uncommon Truth 021 (Oroville, California: The Father's House Church)

170 Orsillo, S. (29/06/2020), 'The blueprint for real world change', The Uncommon Truth 056 (Oroville, California: The Father's House Church)

171 Millar, R., as quoted in Waite, S. (05/10/2022), 'Government should be "last resort" for alleviating poverty', Tory MP tells charities', Civil Society

172 Orsillo, S. (13/04/2020), 'What Jesus says about selflessness', The Uncommon Truth 045 (Oroville, California: The Father's House Church)

173 I'm not going to give the reference because I don't want to embarrass the speaker

174 See, e.g., Mission Frontiers: https://www.missionfrontiers.org/issue/article/what-wesley-practiced-and-preached-about-money

175 Padley, M. and Stone, J. (2023), 'A Minimum Income Standard for the United Kingdom in 2023' (York: Joseph Rowntree Foundation)

176 Trussell Trust and Joseph Rowntree Foundation (27/02/2023), 'Guarantee our Essentials: reforming Universal Credit to ensure we can all afford the essentials in hard times',

https://www.jrf.org.uk/report/guarantee-our-essentials

177 Balboni, C., Bandiera, O., Burgess, R., Ghatak, M. and Heil, A. (2021), 'Why do people stay poor?', National Bureau of Economic Research, Working Paper 29340

178 Balboni, C., Bandiera, O., Burgess, R., Ghatak, M. and Heil, A. (2021), 'Why do people stay poor?', National Bureau of Economic Research, Working Paper 29340

179 Social Exclusion Unit (2004), 'Jobs and Enterprise in Deprived Areas', Office of the Deputy Prime Minister MacDonald and Marsh (2005), 'Disconnected Youth? Growing up in Britain's Poor Neighbourhood', (Palgrave). Fletcher et al (2008), 'Social Housing and Worklessness: Qualitative research findings', DWP Research Report No 521. Prince's Trust (2010), 'Destined for the dole? Breaking the cycle of worklessness in the UK', Prince's Trust and Qa Research. Shildrick et al (2012), 'Are "Cultures of Worklessness" Passed Down the Generations?', Joseph Rowntree Foundation

180 Mullainathan, S. and Shafir, E. (2013), 'Scarcity: why having too little means so much' (London: Allen Lane)

181 Paraphrase of Mullainathan, S. and Shafir, E. (2013), 'Scarcity: why having too little means so much' (London: Allen Lane), p.100

182 Mullainathan, S. and Shafir, E. (2013), 'Scarcity: why having too little means so much' (London: Allen Lane)

CHAPTER 6: THE SIN OF THE PEOPLE

183 Exodus 3-4

184 Barker, A. (2009), 'Make Poverty Personal: taking the poor as seriously as the Bible does', Victoria, Australia: Urban Neighbours of Hope

185 Plass, A. (1988), Snowdon, in *Clearing Away the Rubbish* (Eastbourne: Monarch Publications), adapted from 'Letter to William' in *The Final Boundary*.

186 Luke 12:1

187 Isaiah 1:3

188 Jeremiah 8:6

189 Micah 2:6-7,11, 3:5; Isaiah 30:10

190 Jeremiah 8:7

191 Micah 6:6-8

192 Malachi 1:7-8

193 Malachi 3:8-10

194 Malachi 1:13-14

195 Malachi 2:11

196 Malachi 2:14

197 Malachi 2:17; 3:5,14-15

198 Malachi 1:6; 2:17; 3:8,13

199 Malachi 2:13; 3:15

200 Malachi 2:17

201 Malachi 3:14

202 Malachi 3:5
203 Malachi 2:14-16
204 Malachi 3:5,9
205 Isaiah 26:10
206 Jeremiah 5:24
207 Amos 4:6-11
208 Malachi 3:14
209 Isaiah 1:11-15; 58:2-3
210 Amos 5:21-23
211 Jeremiah 7:4
212 Isaiah 29:13; Jeremiah 7:8
213 Isaiah 48:1
214 Jeremiah 12:2
215 Hosea 12:8
216 Jeremiah 16:10
217 Jeremiah 2:22
218 Jeremiah 7:9-10
219 Jeremiah 8:8
220 Amos 5:24
221 Jeremiah 7:3-11
222 Jeremiah 7:11
223 Isaiah 59:2-4
224 Amos 5:21
225 Isaiah 66:3
226 Jeremiah 9:25-26; Ezekiel 44:9
227 Jeremiah 2:22
228 Isaiah 66:3
229 Hosea 6:6
230 Hosea 12:6
231 Hosea 10:12-13
232 Hosea 14:2-3
233 Isaiah 66:3; Jeremiah 7:21
234 Isaiah 2:6; 57:6-9; 66:3-4; 66:17; Jeremiah 5:7; 7:18

235 Isaiah 2:8; 44:19; Jeremiah 10; 11:10

236 Isaiah 44:19

237 Jeremiah 13:25

238 Isaiah 8:19-10

239 Isaiah 58; Jeremiah 3:4-5; 11:15

240 Jeremiah 3:4b-5a

241 Jeremiah 3:1

242 Jeremiah 3:10-11

243 Ezekiel 23:11

244 Isaiah 3:16

245 Isaiah 5:11-12; 56:11-12

246 Isaiah 28:1,5

247 Isaiah 5:20

248 Isaiah 65:5

249 Jeremiah 17:5

250 Hosea 7:11, 12:1; Isaiah 8:6, Isaiah 20:6, 30:2; Jeremiah
      2:18; 13:21

251 Hosea 2:5

252 Jeremiah 2:13; 17-18

253 Hosea 11:3-4

254 Isaiah 22:8-11; Jeremiah 5:24

255 Jeremiah 5:22-24

256 Hosea 10:13; 13:6

257 Haggai 1:6

258 Haggai 1:4, 7-11

259 Haggai 2:12-14

260 Obadiah 1:3

261 Obadiah 1:11-14

262 Obadiah 1:2-4

263 Jeremiah 5:7-8; 29:23; Ez 22:11

264 Hosea 4:14

265 E.g. Jeremiah 13:25-27

266 Amos 2:7-8

267 See, e.g., Balmford A. et al (2002) 'Economic reasons for conserving wild nature'. Science 297, 950 - 953.

Costanza R et al (1997) 'The value of the world's ecosystem services and natural capital'. Nature 387, 253 - 260.

Dasgupta P (2021) *The economics of biodiversity: The Dasgupta Review*. London: HM Treasury

268 See, e.g., overshootday.org

269 Isaiah 20:5-6

270 Isaiah 14:13, 47:10

271 Isaiah 19:11; 47:12-13

272 Luke 16:1-15

273 Ephesians 4:28

274 Townsend, N. (2009), 'Government and social infrastructure', p. 126, in *God and Government* Spencer, N. and Chaplin, J. (eds.)

275 Ibid. p. 125-6

CHAPTER 7: THE SIN OF THE LEADERS

276 Matthew 21:28-32

277 Jeremiah 21:12

278 Amos 1:3, 6, 9,11,13; 2:1.

The Israelites made a special effort to preserve the bones of the dead, removing them from graves after a year to keep in ossuaries. They believed that the bones of a person were resurrected at the end of time and were the basis for the resurrection body.

279 Amos 2:4

280 Amos 2:6-8

281 Amos 4:1

282 Amos 5:11; 6:4-5

283 Amos 5:11

284 Amos 5:11

285 Amos 5:7

286 Amos 5:10,12

287 Amos 2:12; 7:13

288 Micah 2:1-2

289 Micah 2:8-9

290 Micah 3:2-3

291 Micah 2:2, 8-10

292 Micah 3:2

293 Micah 3:10

294 Amos 2:10-12; 3:1-2

295 Amos 3:7; 4:3,8-11

296 Nahum 1:11

297 Nahum 1:14

298 Nahum 3:4

299 Nahum 3:1

300 Nahum 3:16-17

301 Habakkuk 1:3-4

302 Habakkuk 1:12, 17

303 Habakkuk 1:15-17, 2:5

304 Habakkuk 2:18-19

305 Habakkuk 2:4-5

306 Habakkuk 2:6-17

307 Zechariah 1:3-4

308 Zechariah 7:10, 12

309 Zechariah 7:11-12

310 Zechariah 7:14

311 Zechariah 7:5-6

312 Zechariah 7:9-10; 8:16-17

313 Isaiah 1:16-17, 23; 5:23

314 Jeremiah 6:13; 8:10

315 Isaiah 3:15

316 Isaiah 3:14

317 Jeremiah 22:15-16
318 Isaiah 30:10-12; Jeremiah 22:17
319 Ezekiel 34:17-24
320 Isaiah 32:7
321 Isaiah 32:6
322 Isaiah 58:6-7; Jeremiah 21:12
323 Jeremiah 7:5-6
324 Jeremiah 22:3, 9
325 Isaiah 56:2
326 Jeremiah 9:8; James 2:16
327 Jeremiah 9:9
328 Jeremiah 6:20
329 Jeremiah 6:20
330 Micah 6:8
331 Micah 6:6-7
332 Jeremiah 9:26
333 Ezekiel 22
334 Exodus 20:12
335 Exodus 21:17
336 Proverbs 26:2
337 Matthew 5:21-23
338 Leviticus 19:33
339 Isaiah 58:9b-10a
340 Leviticus 17:18-19
341 Jeremiah 5:31; 6:14; 8:10-11; 14:13-14
342 Jeremiah 5:12-13
343 Jeremiah 6:10; 17
344 Malachi 2:5-6
345 Malachi 2:2
346 Zephaniah 3:4
347 Malachi 2:8
348 Malachi 2:8
349 Micah 1:6

350 Zephaniah 3:1

351 Zephaniah 3:3

352 Zephaniah 3:3-4

353 Isaiah 1:23; 5:23; Jeremiah 22:17

354 Isaiah 19:21; 59:4

355 Jeremiah 5:28

356 Jeremiah 28-29

357 Ezekiel 34:2b

358 Micah 3:11

359 Micah 7:3

360 Micah 6:10-11, 7:3

361 Micah 3:9

362 Micah 7:4

363 Micah 3:11

364 Micah 2:3-5, 10, 6:13-15

365 Micah 3:4

366 Micah 6:13-15

367 Shaw, I. (2021), *Evangelicals and Social Action: from John Wesley to John Stott* (IVP)

368 Rivers, J. (2009), 'The nature and role of government in the Bible', p. 49, in *God and Government*, Spencer, N. and Chaplin, J. (eds.) (London: SPCK)

369 Spencer and Chaplin (2009), *God and Government.*

370 Galatians 5:9-10

371 Spencer and Chaplin (2009), *God and Government*

372 Romans 13:4

373 1 Peter 2:14

374 *God and Government*, chapter 4

375 Lowe, R. (2005), *The Welfare State in Britain since 1945*, 3rd edition (Basingstoke, Palgrave Macmillan)

376 For arguments against capitalism as a social good, see in particular work by Jason Hickel, e.g. Sullivan, D. and Hickel, J. (2022), 'Capitalism and

extreme poverty: A global analysis of real wages, human height, and mortality since the long 16th century', *World Development* 161:106026
Doi: 10.1016/j.worlddev.2022.106026

377 Lowe, *The Welfare State in Britain since 1945*.

378 Ostry, J., Loungani, P. and Furceri, D. (2016), 'Neoliberalism: oversold?', *Finance and Development* 53(2)

379 Lowe, *The Welfare State in Britain since 1945*

380 Wilkinson and Pickett, *The Spirit Level*

381 Van Kersbergen, K. (2017), 'The welfare state in Europe' in *The search for Europe: contrasting approaches*, Open Mind, BBVA

382 Barr, N. (2001), *The Welfare State as Piggy Bank: Information, Risk, Uncertainty, and the Role of the State* (Oxford: Oxford University Press)

383 Kees Van Keersbergen (2016), The Welfare State in Europe in *The Search for Europe: Contrasting Approaches*, BBVA

384 Van der Wel and Halvorsen (2015)

385 Kees Van Keersbergen (2016), The Welfare State in Europe in *The Search for Europe: Contrasting Approaches*, BBVA

CHAPTER 8: GOD'S ECONOMY: DEBT AND WORK LAWS

386 Orsillo, S. (18/05/2020), 'Does Jesus command us to forgive?' The Uncommon Truth 050 (Oroville, California: The Father's House Church)

387 Numbers 26

388 1 Kings 21:1-16

389 Leviticus 25:35; Deuteronomy 15:7-11

390 Deuteronomy 15:7-9

391 Burnside, J. (2010), *God, Justice and Society* (Oxford: Oxford University Press), p. 223

392 Luke 7:47

393 Matthew 20:1-16

394 Luke 6:34-35

395 Deuteronomy 24:12-13

396 Deuteronomy 24:6

397 Deuteronomy 24:10-11

398 Exodus 22:25; Leviticus 25:36-37; Deuteronomy 23:19

399 Leviticus 19:9, Deuteronomy 24:19-22

400 Deuteronomy 23:25-26

401 Meeks, D.M. (1989), *God the Economist* (Minneapolis: Fortress)

402 Leviticus 25:23-34

403 Hence the eighteenth-century poem 'They hang the man and flog the woman /Who steals the goose from off the common /Yet let the greater villain loose /That steals the common from the goose.' There are more verses on the same theme.

404 Leviticus 25:29-30

405 Leviticus 19:13; 25:35, 39, 43, 46, 53; Deuteronomy 24:15

406 Leviticus 19:13

407 Leviticus 25:37

408 Deuteronomy 15:12-15

409 Micah 3:9

410 Townsend, N. (2009), 'Government and Social Infrastructure' in *God and Government*

411 Ibid., 120 - 1

412 Siegrist, J., Rosskam, E. and Leka, S. (2012), 'Work and worklessness: Final report of the Task group on employment and working conditions, including occupation, unemployment and migrant workers',

Review of social determinants of health and the health divide in the WHO European Region (Denmark: World Health Organisation)

413 Stuckler, D., Basu, S., Suhrcke, M., Coutts, A., McKee, M. (2009), 'The public health effect of economic crises and alternative policy responses in Europe: an empirical analysis', *The Lancet* 374(9686):315-323 doi: 10.1016/S0140-6736(09)61124-7

414 See, e.g., MacDonald, R. and Marsh, J. (2005), *Disconnected Youth? Growing up in Britain's Poor Neighbourhood* (London: Palgrave Macmillan). Shildrick, MacDonald, Furlong, Roden and Crow (2012), 'Are "Cultures of Worklessness" Passed Down the Generations?'

415 As of April 2024, after-housing income support for jobseekers is £90.80 a week. The Joseph Rowntree Foundation calculated that, in 2023, a single person needed £95/week in order to not be destitute. This means that benefits are below destitution level, even before a jobseeker has to use some of their £90.80 to top-up inadequate support for Council Tax and rent, and to deal with inflation since 2023.
Fitzpatrick, S., Bramley, G., Treanor, M., Blenkinsopp, J., McIntyre, J., Johnsen, S., McMordie, L. (2023), Destitution in the UK 2023 (York: Joseph Rowntree Foundation).

416 Indeed, there is plenty of evidence that current 'work-search' requirements are damaging. See, e.g., Jones, K., Wright, S., Scullion, L. (2024), 'The Impact of Welfare Conditionality on Experiences of Job Quality', Work, Employment and Society. Doi: 10.1177/09500170231219

Welfare Conditionality Project (2018) Final Findings Report.

417 Isaiah 32:7; Micah 2:1-2

418 Hafner, M., Taylor, J., Pankowska, P., Stepanek ,M., Nataraj, S. and van Stolk, C. (2016), 'The impact of the National Minimum Wage on employment: a meta-analysis', A report for the UK Low Pay Commission, RAND Europe

419 Housing completions, Communities and Local Government, 1950 to 2010

420 Scoop.me (10/11/2020) Finland is the only country in Europe where homelessness is in decline. https://scoop.me/housing-first-finland-homelessness/

421 Marmot, M., Allen, J., Goldblatt, P., Boyce, T., McNeish, D., Grady, M. and Geddes, I. (2010), 'Fair society, healthy lives: The Marmot Review', Strategic review of health inequalities in England post-2010, Institute of Health Equity.

422 Marmot, M. (2015), *The Health Gap: the challenge of an unequal world* (London: Bloomsbury Publishing).

423 Romans 13:4

424 *God and Government*

CHAPTER 9: TRUE CHRISTIANITY

425 Matthew 23:24; see also Luke 11:46

426 Matthew 11:30

427 Avoth i.15

428 Luke 11:39; see also Matthew 23:25

429 James 1:27

430 Isaiah 58:6-7

431 Jeremiah 22:3,15-16

432 Philippians 2:12

433 Luke 16:2

434 James 2:19

435 Matthew 7:21

436 Matthew 5:16

437 Matthew 7:24

438 Matthew 7:21, 12:50

439 Matthew 21:31

440 Matthew 25:34-36

441 Matthew 7:21

442 Matthew 7:24-27

443 Matthew 12:50

444 Luke 6:35

445 1 John 2:4

446 1 John 3:10

447 James 2:17; 1 John 3:18

448 1 John 2:3,5-6

449 Matthew 7:21-23

450 Deuteronomy 10:18

451 1 Samuel 2:8

452 Isaiah 1:17

453 Jeremiah 22:16

454 Proverbs 14:31

455 Proverbs 19:17

456 Matthew 25:34-36

457 Isaiah 58:4

458 Proverbs 21:13

459 Amos 5:21-23

460 Isaiah 32:7

461 Sander, M. (2009), *Justice: what's the right thing to do?* (New York: Farrar, Straus and Giroux)

462 Friedman, M. and Friedman, R. D. (1980), *Free to Choose* (New York: Harcourt Brace Jovanovich)

463 Friedman, M. (13/09/1970,) 'The Social Responsibility of Business is to Increase its Profits', *The New York Times*

464 Fitzpatrick, S., Bramley, G., Treanor, M., Blenkinsopp, J., McIntyre, J., Johnsen, S., McMordie, L. (2023) *Destitution in the UK 2023* (York: Joseph Rowntree Foundation).

465 Luke 15:3-7

466 Luke 15:23

467 Matthew 20:1-16

468 Marmot, M. (2015), *The Health Gap: the challenge of an unequal world.*

469 Luke 5:31-32

470 Luke 7:47